CHINA

Living and Teaching in Shandong

Don Patter

To all of my friends in China

British Library Cataloguing In Publication Data

A Record of this Publication is available

from the British Library

ISBN 978-1-84685-560-3

First Published 2007 by

Exposure Publishing, an imprint of Diggory Press

Diggory Press Ltd, Three Rivers, Minions,

Liskeard, Cornwall, PL14 5LE, UK

Affiliated to:

Diggory Press, Inc. of Goodyear, Arizona, USA

WWW.DIGGORYPRESS.COM

China – Living and Teaching in Shandong

You should read this book for one of three reasons:

- If you are visiting the country for enjoyment or to work it will prepare you for the highs and lows of living in this modern/ancient country. While everyone who lives in the country will have a unique experience I believe, from talking to many other westerners, that my experience was broadly representative of what one might expect.

- If you despair of life in the west this will give you some hope and also begin to answer some of the problems that beset Europe and the States at the moment. China may have problems of its own but one thing that it does have is relative stability based on strong family and community values.

- If you have a general interest in how people live in different cultures and a delight in reading about the land that shapes them.

Each section is roughly in chronological order, is self-contained and reflects a personal response at the time of writing. Hopefully what one loses in continuity one gains in freshness of observation. My thanks are due to Charlotte Garth for her contribution and to Peng Huibing for his help in translation

December 2006

4

ARRIVAL

The small child looked up at me his brow furrowed in concentration. "Twelve" I prompted correcting the v & the I which had become interposed. "Ah . ." he breathed gratefully "Thank-you master." Another successful lesson I thought as I packed up my things and made for the tea-house next to the lily pond thoughtfully provided by the school. I'll try the *secret heavens lotus tea* today I mused as I planned my next strategy with the class.

Well, no actually. It isn't quite like that here. I am teaching English to 10 & 11 year olds: there are 40-45 in the class and the sole resource is a couple of books from Longman. Much of the work is repetition – I've had four weeks of reinforcing a vocabulary of twenty words and with nine groups following the same course that's an awful lot of repetition. I see each group twice a week – eighteen lessons of forty minutes.

So that's the bonus – only twelve hours teaching a week, with minimal preparation or marking, and also no travelling time as I live on the campus although, as you may imagine, that isn't perfect either. With a dawn chorus of awakening children at 6.00 I have no need for an alarm. My earliest lesson starts at 10.00 and latest ends at 4.30. Lunch lasts for two and a half hours.

The children are mostly open and receptive, given that their attention often wanders. It is hard work communicating with 40+ without the benefit of the meta-language of teaching (stop that, sit down etc.) and in two lessons a week memories and pronunciation suffer. One scary thing is how similar they are to UK students, how you can see a "type" – the slightly over-friendly pupil, the eager, the want-to-be-seen-to-be-participating-without-much-idea pupil, the cocky pupil: teacher's radar! However they are extremely affable with no malice. There's no posturing, insults (as far as I know), no litter, no chewing gum, no defiance, no damage: it's not quite education nirvana but . . well, you get the picture.

Lessons, interwoven with ten minute breaks, are signaled by a burst of fairground music which has pupils instantly scurrying to class. They apologise if late, there is little animosity shown to each other, they all, two thousand of them, live together in relative harmony twenty-four hours a day for five days of the week; on Saturday morning they go home after sweeping and cleaning the campus, returning on Sunday evening.

The site probably occupies the same footprint as a school in England with half the pupils but is more compact as it has to provide accommodation and a running track. Many of the buildings are four or five storeys. As befits its status entrance is through a controlled gate into a grand courtyard with sculpture and fountain. Busts of educational worthies line the route. Many of the schools here have quite elaborate entrances. It means that Education is valued. As anywhere the architecture betokens the worth with which the institution is endowed. Improving slogans can be found on the exterior - "We educate our students to become well-balanced citizens of the future" - and inside classrooms. A massive digital display carries the principal's thought for the day.

I have never been handed a form list – they don't exist. Holidays and teaching come and go at a whim it seems. I didn't get a timetable until the afternoon before I started – and then had to work through the first weekend. We had a Friday off and two days the following week. Not even the admin staff knows what is happening. It seems that the the principal waits for a phone call from the communist party telling him when to open and when to close.

I had resigned from my post in the UK. For years schools had been operating in a sort of educational wonderland. My concept of a profession is of a body that is largely self-governing and has a strong ethic to pursue its aims. A professional is someone who has a vocation which commits them to those aims and who is involved in furthering them for the good, in the case of the teaching profession, of children's education. "Professionalism" is now a piece of double-speak which means a foot-soldier in the classroom governed by "initiatives" which have more in common with advertising strap-lines than serious ideas. The commercial paradigm is extended into the idea of schools having to compete with each other for customers, and their "product" - in this case successful exam students – quantified and set out like a company profit sheet. Common-sense suggests that you cannot treat teachers like shelf-stackers or children like tins of peas.

This process had happened over a period of about fifteen years and at the same time society changed too. The number of single-parent families increased and the time that parents spent with children decreased. Media images and new technologies gave authority and power to the way young people operated in the vacuum left by the desertion of their parents. This was reinforced by debates and laws about the rights of young people that resulted in a situation where power and control no longer resided with teachers in schools. I am not right-wing, I am not hungry for power, my training was during the time of the "Child-centred" approach. In many classes I was becoming a zoo-keeper. I was keeping children in check from hurting each other or maintaining a semblance of social decency. Little of educational worth was happening.

The cost of this was tremendous stress on the teaching staff, many of whom needed periods of absence as respite for the strain endured. There are only so many creative ways that you can find to cope with being told to fuck off by a small child or deal with the inter-pupil feuds that spring like soap-operas out of nowhere. The anguish was there also of watching the decent kids deal with all of this too. They could brazen it out and become outsiders in their own classroom, or they could join in the fray to maintain street-credibility. Some managed to become invisible, to keep their head below the parapet while the mayhem raged. Meanwhile the government either powerless or perversely looking in the other direction demanded better results or better teaching as if it was bad teaching that had caused bad behaviour. I resigned because I no longer wanted to be part of this educational wonderland.

The job in China was heaven sent. It would enable me to distance myself from the insanity of the UK and see things from a new perspective. I would be in a different culture and experiencing another way of doing things. I knew I would be meeting children who had incredibly different life experiences from those encountered in the west. It would be a sabbatical worth far more than an MA or UK based work experience even if it had been on offer. There would be a new climate, new language, new friends to deal with and some travel. One two-hour telephone interview and a twenty-one hour flight later here I was in Weifang

Weifang (*Way-fang*) is a "small" town of six million within the larger district it serves. It lies fairly centrally in the great plain that has been scoured dead flat by the Yellow river over hundreds of years in the eastern province of

Shandong and an eight hour train ride south of Beijing. If you can visualise China as a chicken looking to the east, Weifang is in the neck region. As with hundreds of such towns all over China nothing particularly distinguishes it. It has grown from two walled cities that faced each other across the river. Now only part of one wall remains on one side of a sham river. The flow has been dammed in a great reservoir 20 km south of the city near to the small airport and the riverbed serves as a scenic lake for about 5 or 6 kilometers within the city, a pleasant place to fish and wash and walk. Look over the bridge that carries DongFeng street and there you can see the holding dam and a dry bed beyond. DongFeng is the principal street running east/west for some twelve kilometers through the heart of the town and bears a climatic significance: literally translated it means east wind and it is this that blows along the road, sometimes cooling, sometimes frozen but usually grittily laden with the fumes from the fertiliser factory on the outskirts.

Like most Chinese cities Weifang is laid out in a grid pattern with roads stretching away in a predictably straight line into the dusty distance. Like most Chinese cities it is growing and renewing itself, almost before your eyes, the trucks and cranes performing a ceaseless dance. Buildings are demolished, vast holes are excavated, concrete is poured and within a frighteningly short time the townscape is changed forever – or until the next cycle of renewal. In parts of the city some roads are still dirt tracks with piles of rubbish and goats and chickens scurrying around. Old country courtyard houses still exist in what is now the middle of the city, some of them truncated by a new road or development. Like ink on blotting paper the margins of the city are moving out wards in all directions with indecent haste. Rose, the first person to meet me at the airport and who becomes an invaluable aid throughout my time here, can remember going to visit her grandparents in fields with gardens and trees barely fifteen years ago when she was a child. They haven't moved but they would now have to travel several blocks before they reached the countryside.

The city seems smarter to the east of the river – newer shops, grander hotels, showy bank buildings and at the end of Donfeng street the new university buildings although the institution itself is now thirty proud years old. In the other direction streets that need re-paving, smaller shop frontages and meaner restaurants. In most parts of the city there are parks and open spaces. The grandest is probably the substantial Peoples' Park in the centre with pristine lawns and water channels. More modest spaces are found tucked between blocks or on odd corners. They are all well used whatever the weather and especially in the evenings. The roads are wide enough for three lanes of motor traffic in each direction with an extra fourth lane for bicycles. Traffic moves lazily controlled at intersections by lights which include a countdown display to point of change. Sometimes a vehicle moves in the wrong direction for the carriageway and often a road user turns onto a road without checking that their way is clear. Sometimes there are accidents but there is no rage, no road rage and usually not even a sign of exasperation. Horns are sounded certainly, but merely to warn other users of your presence. There is rarely any congestion.

Certain streets have developed their own markets and on my early exploratory walks of the city these were my favourite. Vegetables and fruit are spilled onto the pavements in the lesser markets or arranged on stalls in the more grown-up ones. Charcoal barbecues and gas stoves are poised to cook instant meals and the raw ingredients are chopped ready next to them in glass cabinets. In glass cabinets too are piled up massacres of roasted duck carcasses. Sometimes the raw ingredient –

a goat – stands tethered to a tree. The stall-holders rarely harass the passers-by but sit for hours patiently. I always love to walk these streets because of their colour and vibrancy and because of the unexpected such as an unusual vegetable or street-food. Other side-streets have less charm and seem to have lost all self-respect with crumbling apartments, fetid puddles, billowing plastic rubbish but still in their own way fascinating.

The first morning that I awoke in Weifang my throat felt like the inside of a factory chimney despite the fact that it was high summer. After that I kept the window shut at all times. In the winter when everything was heated by the dirty coal the thick smoke poured from crazy steel stacks into the atmosphere at a rate that was clearly a risk for people and planet. In my apartment even with windows shut a black film of soot would settle over the course of a week on the shiny ceramic floor; surfaces would need wiping and window sills left for a month would accumulate a layer of black powder. It didn't pay to think too hard about all of this. If it was arriving on horizontal surfaces with such efficiency then it must be constantly in the air – the air that was going in my lungs twenty-four hours a day. Next to the main gate of the fertiliser factory a block away a stream ran under *Dongfeng* Street eventually coming to the fields to the north of the city. For the whole of its course it was stinking and dead. It seems that discharge into water courses was not controlled in China. How sad to think that in a country where so much is controlled – the number of children that a couple may have, what you can access on the internet, where you live – pollution seems to attract no effective controls at all. I have known foreigners to be relocated from cities because of the poor air quality and it was common in winter in Weifang to see people wearing protective masks. One tributary of the *Yangtze* river is so polluted with effluent from waste-paper treatment that locals who border it are falling sick with the cancer that it induces.

As a westerner walking the streets you attracted a lot of attention. I remember a novelty toy that was popular when I was younger: a rotating figurine of a man would kiss a stationary woman as he passed her, his neck would swivel as he came near her, their gazes would hold, their lips touched and they remained locked into each others eyes until the magnets which enabled all of this were out of range. It was exactly like this in Weifang; as you passed someone you and they would continue on your respective paths but their heads would turn and track you well beyond what was a decent or seemly stare. When cyclists did this I always expected them to end up knocking into someone because their attention was diverted but they never did. One English word that all Chinese people knew was "ha-loo" and often you were greeted with this, but usually *after* they had passed you. Any response on your part was likely to elicit a series of embarrassed giggles. With all of its western airs - modern cars, shops that sold mobile telephones, department stores – it seemed odd that east/west integration had progressed so little. However, centuries of Chinese isolation and poor mobility meant that in 2006 this was still a frontier town in that many of the residents still had country mud on their shoes and would not have encountered white faces other than in a few films. I suppose at first all of this was a bit intimidating but you learned to treat it as simple curiosity.

Plumbing

Forget the heat of the day, forget the friendliness of the population, forget the fascinating endless street markets, just concentrate for a moment on plumbing. Why is it that so many countries have simply not got their heads round such a basic requirement of civilization? One does not appreciate the solidness of British pipe and ceramic until one sees the opposition. Two things mark the British versions as superior: designs that make sense and work, and robustness of material and manufacture.

Here for less than two weeks and already several wrestles with the stuff. The device in my cistern which releases the water into the toilet is a simple flap valve. It is lifted by a lever operated by a plunger and it was broken. The on-site janitor "mended" it by attaching a length of string directly to the flap and telling me to pull it. Well I'd already worked that one out as a temporary measure. So off to likely looking shops and found a replacement for the broken plunger in the second one I came to. I Fitted it with some difficulty because leaning on the toilet lid is ill advised as it has the strength of a poppadom. It now worked but, being what it is, the flap sometimes did not close so that water was slowly but gently running through.

Next, because the float for the shut-off valve was too big for the cistern, it lodged against the top and did not shut off the supply – result a sliver of water constantly across the floor. I have to isolate the supply to the cistern to enjoy a dry floor. Next the water heater leaked furiously, and if the electrics are as good as the plumbing, probably dangerously too. The janitor managed to cure two out of the three leaks. The shower water does not drain properly and when I investigate I find it soaks into an open hole: I am wary of looking into that one!

The overflow for the sink is not connected, nor for the toilet, the tap's chrome is rusting, the tiles are cracked and lifting and seem to be home to a species of small worm – I could go on. Why can't they design and build plumbing that bloody works? I remember this in Peru and I've encountered it in France and Spain. Never mind democracy, if only we had exported the concept of the syphonic cistern.

Think of me next time you go to the toilet.

I am taking the road northwards out of the city. For about fifteen minutes there is quite heavy traffic on the road and grit in the air until we find the river, unexpectedly full of water with a good track alongside. As we come to bridges we find that the edges of the roads over them are covered in sweetcorn drying. In some places the workers are separating the corn from the cobs and there are also makeshift beds with covers set up to guard them. The track is good for a long way as it is elevated above the surrounding countryside and we look down on densely cultivated allotments. Occasionally there is a cemetery or a small lake with fishermen relaxing. Every so often there are dwellings which seem to be courtyard houses amongst the fields. The track is good because it has been planted with trees so there is shade too. At some point the water level falls, disappears completely and the crops take over the riverbed too.

Eventually the track bears west and we are now navigating our return – keeping the afternoon sun on our left. Apart from the crops themselves, which are planted very densely, the land is featureless and flat. Even though we are in the agricultural countryside we can often glimpse the foggy outlines of a building project. The tracks are now in the heart of the forests of sweetcorn, apples, and smaller crops but are unpredictable. A new one appears to stretch forever but suddenly comes to a T-junction or bears in the wrong direction or just peters out. Eventually we get it right and see a large construction site that formed a landmark for us on the way out. People are working everywhere and we pass through some villages, all with mud tracks and seemingly no shops.

The city looms, roads suddenly look business-like and we are back in the fumes and dust. Still not home yet, but one or two lucky guesses and more roads covered in drying sweetcorn and we arrive safely.

I think China must have a shoe mountain or maybe Imelda Marcos was having a boot (!) sale. *Weifang* has a market for everything: electronics, art, antiques, tea, clothes, second-hand goods. Napoleon sneered that the English were a nation of shopkeepers but he had not seen China. I found an enormous building with a thousand tiny lock-up stalls – each selling shoes. How can they do it? It must have been 200 yards long with three or four aisles as well as cross-aisles and every single stall selling shoes. The same shoes at the same prices. Not far away there were other markets with fish flopping around, meat and vegetables but probably with more vendors than buyers. My favourite was The People's market which is enormous and sells almost everything that you could possibly want aside from food. By the river there is a pet market with fish, dogs, cats small stripy mammals which I later found out were a type of squirrel, tree frogs, and crickets in cages. I tried out my Chinese "*Ker ee jao jao syeung ma*?" She smiled at me "Oh you want to take a photo do you?" Doh! At least I made myself understood.

I spent time in the new park - a year ago this was a construction site. They've made a good job of it. Serpentine paths with grassy borders and well-planted beds. Mature trees which have been transplanted are carefully nurtured with straw wrapping and props to keep them upright until their root system develops. Water is to be found everywhere, in pools, streams and waterfalls. It comes complete with sweepers fastidiously sweeping and picking up every grain of refuse, and uniformed park police who blow whistles at you if you venture on to the grass. The river beside it is a scenic device. There is not enough water in China to allow it to flow so it is dammed about a kilometer downstream. On Sundays the park also comes complete with pre-nuptial photographers, brides and grooms who use the garden setting and buildings as romantic settings for photographs which are prepared in advance of the ceremony itself. A solitary angler plays the flute, older men sit encircled by the imprisoned songbirds they have brought in cages.

TRAVELLING IN SHANDONG

Imagine the concourse of a bus station somewhere in provincial England. A Chinese gentleman – say about 54 years old – not noticeably distressed or confused has been waiting for some time on one of the busiest days of the year. Despite this, officials who learn of his wait from other passengers and realise he has little English, give him a chair and then show him onto the bus when it turns up. I would love to think that this would happen. It certainly happened to me on several occasions. Once I was ushered to the head of a queue for a cable-car, and once the destination of a bus was re-assigned for my benefit (and a number of other passengers). If you remember the notorious case involving immigrants I fear that in England we would give the Chinese gentleman a pound for a day's labour, a rip-tide and then leave him to drown.

On that first day's long travel, entering *Qufu* (Choo-foo) at dusk was a bonus. Ornamental dragons, the bridges, the roofs of the gateways on the walled city were picked out with ropelights. The next day traversing the wall was an excellent way of knowing the city. It is wide enough to drive a bus along and there was no one on it. You are part of the city, but no one sees you and you see everything. The grotesque modern buildings, little old courtyards, schools, markets, workers, children and surrounding moat. If the Rough Guide is to be believed it is 8km all the way round.

A friend of mine used to tell a joke – you can see the glint in his eye as he prepares and then adopts a cod-Chinese accent: "Confucius, he say rape impossible: woman with skirt up run faster than man with trouser down" *Qufu* is the home of Confucius or Kong Fu and although I don't think he ever actually said that, everything that he did say can be found here on posters and in books. Although of lowly birth he spawned a dynasty of rulers, the *Kongs*, that had a tight grip over the town right up until the 1940's. What they left were two awe-inspiring edifices: their mansion and a temple to Confucian thought. Both are similar in layout and comprise a number of separate buildings arranged around courtyards and approached from the South through a series of increasingly imposing gateways and with a labyrinth of passages. Only the most favoured servants could enter the family apartments which had separate dwellings for the Duke, his wife and his concubines. Water was delivered via a trough that was set in an aperture in the wall. This meant that when a fire broke out in the inner sanctum only twelve of the five hundred servants were allowed to deal with it; consequently it raged for three days! It is eerie to consider that less than seventy years ago the *Kongs* were leading a life full of feudal power, ritual and privilege and yet living in conditions more akin to those of an English Lord in Arthurian times. With the Japanese invasion in 1940 they fled to Taiwan. The great line came to an end – except that nearly everyone in Qufu claims to be related to the family and to prove it several pages of the phone book are still devoted to people with the name Kong.

A mixed forest several hundred years old is a rare sight. Every inch of land for the last 400km that I have been traveling has been intensively cultivated and teems with humanity. This is a place to relieve the senses too from the hardness of city life. There are people but not often. The twisted cedars drip, the Jays gather and chatter, the soil smells and feels good beneath the feet. Its romance is completed with the presence of thousands of Kongs – dead ones. This is their graveyard and it is not possible to move in this vast enclosed forest without seeing a tombstone or monument. It feels so good that I spend the whole day here. Sometimes the tracks double back, but more often lead to a new tomb such as stone tortoise-like creature with the inscription carried on an upright stone on its back. Some of the grander monuments are at the end of an avenue lined with pairs of guardians – seated horsemen, sentient swordsmen facing each other. There are also some simple earth covered graves strewn with charred paper lanterns still evident from a recent ceremony.

I range freely through the forest but at some point there is the unmistakable gabble of people and the amplified quack of tour guides (why are they always female?) Drawing reluctantly nearer I realize I have arrived at the tomb of Confucius himself. The guided tours and day-trippers come straight here and go out again completely missing the immense forest. There is a temple, a headstone and a mound of earth. It is very busy and very odd. Confucius' philosophy is patriarchal and feudal and yet here is modern communist China paying reverence to him. Do they know how much his philosophy is at variance with modern China? He is 2500 years old and he is yesterday's man.

At 1545 metres *Taishan* is in the order of Snowdon. I remember climbing Snowdon through the damp trees and dripping rocks through mist, past sheep and then the steamy fetid shock of hundreds of people crammed into the shop at the top which rather detracted from the wilderness experience. No shock here though as thousands of people from babies to octogenarians were climbing *Taishan* today and all were crammed about me all the way. Unlike Snowdon the route is well paved and stepped for the whole 8km ascent. In addition you can't go more than 500m without encountering a toilet, trinket stall or temple. If you think this is travel writer's hyperbole, it isn't. Despite the crowds the mountain is still beautiful with streams, crags with pines, waterfalls and at the top marvelous views softened by the afternoon heat-haze.

Each temple on the way and at the top is devoted to a particular deity including *Taishan* himself. The gods of these temples are a mixed bunch but spring from the teachings of Buddha. You enter a courtyard with buildings around the side for monks to sleep in and in the centre facing South is a building like a large and very well built garden shed. Inside, in the gloom is a giant model or effigy of the god, sometimes severe and dressed in fine robes, or if it was Buddha himself, with a great grin on his face and with an enormous pot belly all in gold. In front of him is a large box into which people put money. Giant bronze vessels stand in front of the inner chambers containing the images, in which supplicants place bundles of smoking incense. Some of the effigies are attended by monks who sound a note intermittently on a small brass bowl. Again the wonder at such devotion from an officially non-religious society unless it is tied up with superstition. And talking of superstition, tradition holds that anyone who climbs the mountain will live to be a hundred. So take that - Teacher's Pensions!!

Although it was hard going and full of people, I could still enjoy the scenery – limestone crags, pine trees, streams and waterfalls. One teahouse on the way was furnished with tables made from weirdly shaped trunks and roots found on the mountain making it look like a fairy grotto. Because it is a holy mountain many important people have climbed it and so there are many stories connected with it. One emperor who climbed it had so many servants attending him that when he was at the top, there were still servants starting the climb 8km away. Another one was so grateful to some pine trees that gave him shelter from the rain that he promoted them to high-ranking officials in his court. Yet another Emperor who was carried up and down on a donkey did the same for the beast when it eventually dropped dead exhausted. Previous important climbers – such as emperors - have left their mark and their thoughts in the form of giant inscriptions chiseled in the rocks and painted red.

The last part of the climb was the hardest and I was very grateful to reach "Heaven's Gate". Here were yet more thousands of people milling about several shops, restaurants and temples. There is even a hotel at the top. Everything that is sold or used up here has to be carried. This keeps employed a team of men whom I saw with yokes slung with boxes of beer or other goods going up, or rubbish coming down. Apparently they do this three times a day, six days a week; it takes its toll and by the age of thirty many have back deformities. I was lucky with the weather and had some good views despite the heat-haze.

Having climbed under my own steam I decided to take the cable car down to the halfway point. Like thousands of other people. Resigned to waiting in the queue snaking round the mountain, I had just got my ticket when a uniformed official stepped forward, ushered me out of the throng of waiting people and TOLD me to go to the head of the queue – and this because I am a foreigner! I am afraid I accepted. As a Westerner I am highly visible in China and stick out more than black people do in England. Cyclists slow down and gaze curiously at me. People playing cards in the street stop their game to watch me pass. Some greet me with

"Hello" and then giggle when I return the greeting. Some of them stop and talk to practise their English.

In fact it would be true to say that as well as the mountain that day the other tourist attraction was – me. Absolute strangers asked if they could be photographed with me. Body hair is rare on Chinese men (and women too I expect) so another sight to delight them with an unbuttoned shirt to facilitate ventilation, was my hairy chest. Up until the last twenty minutes of my descent I thought I was the only foreigner on Taishan but on the way down I heard the familiar shout of "Hello, hello." But this time the Chinese girl was accompanied by an English couple who were teaching in a town about two hours from my base. The girl, Amy, lived once at a small village north of Shrewsbury from where I used to buy flour. Her mother used to teach at my neighbouring school. Confucius climbed the mountain once and when he reached the top was reported to have said "How small the world is" I don't know exactly what he was thinking but I agree with him.

You probably won't have heard of *Qingdao* (Shing-dow) unless you are keen on Olympic yachting as the city is hosting the maritime events in 2008. If you are an Asian beer aficionado you will have seen the alternative spelling "*Tsingdao*" on China's best known beer which is brewed here.

It was not an auspicious start as the taxi driver wanted to charge me twice the regular fare from the bus station, claiming that the meter didn't work. Thankfully the car ground to a halt with a flat tyre, I escaped and a more honest driver delivered me safely to the monument to kitsch that was the *Lu Bin Yuan* Hotel. After a slight problem with the power supply in the room a phone call was not unexpected; neither was the fact that I couldn't understand it. Thinking that the receptionist was checking that I had electricity I thought nothing further of it. A half hour later the door bell went and thinking how jolly attentive the staff were to ensure my stay went smoothly I opened the door expecting to find the janitor; instead there was a pretty, nicely dressed young woman complete with handbag and smile. This was Trixie and I had apparently asked her to come to my room. No I didn't and yes I did ask her to leave! Speaking to someone the next day it seems that this little extra service is a common feature of hotels here. The following evening when the phone rang I left it alone.

Laoshan is a fantastic wild area to the East of the city with a paved way to the summit and plenty to feast the eye on; temples, rock, pines and cedars, waterfalls and tremendous views of the Yellow Sea glistening in the October sun. At the summit a jumble of boulders taxed ingenuity – whether it was better to leap across from one to another or crawl under and around. In a lotus pool insipid frogs floated fully stretched out as if frozen in mid-leap. Frogs – and lizards and snakes - have a thin time of it here, for if they escape being eaten they end up as dried skins on the souvenir stalls that I saw on the way up.

There is an aquarium in the city but you wonder why, as most restaurants have banks of tanks which house all sorts of regular and some irregular specimens of sea-life, all ready for customers to make their choice. I chose a dish of some indeterminate feathery vegetable steeped in chili and vinegar and after my meal I did my bit for the Anglo-Sino relationship as a vegetarian by going up to the tanks and tutting disapprovingly to the waiters – who of course giggled. The streets around were seething with life. One street was thick with markets; beer street was announced by a giant neon arch of light which simulated the stream of liquid from bottle to glass; the *Tsingdao* Beer factory with silos and vats imaginatively constructed as if they were giant beer cans; a park under a flyover manic with noise and activity which included: two karaoke performers, a percussion group, ballroom dancing, Tai Chi, an artist extolling the virtues of his craft, men and boys on parallel bars, men behind beach-style windbreaks playing cards and pool tables. The only person that I could understand was a deaf-mute.

Qingdao is a modern city as my nineteenth floor morning view of flyovers and skyscrapers made plain. The beauty of it, apart from the wildness of *Laoshan* and the coast, is the abundance of parks and the remains of the German quarter. For *Qingdao* a hundred years ago, was to the Germans, what Hong Kong was to the British. Mercifully winding tree-lined streets run between stolid Teutonic constructions – a real antidote to the brutally modern functionalism of straight roads and concrete that defines the modern Chinese City. Shamefully many of these lovely houses are in serious decline and will disappear into the voracious maw of the developers within the next ten years unless their value is recognized.

The seafront could almost have been anywhere in the world. Sunday strollers out for a bit of leisure, the ubiquitous food and trinket stalls, boat excursions and families on the beach and in the rock pools. On the pier that led to the small pavilion, symbol of the city, were musicians, fortune-tellers, photographers and contortionists. A large crowd was gathered around a very solemn young man who was kneeling upright, head bowed with a large tract in Chinese in front of him held down with stones in the light breeze. Apparently he had a deceased father, his mother was disabled and needed care and he was begging for funds to attend university. I wonder whether someone in his position in the UK would be any better off.

Rattling back off the motorway after the two hour journey, as bits of the city fell into place, it was interesting to feel how at home it felt to be back in *Weifang*; the comfortable familiarity of knowing roads cycled and paths walked. Also a slight regret for a good weekend ended. But I have to say there was none of that figured dread of the coming week that spoilt such returns to school life in the UK.

WILLIAM

Sinolook is the up-market department store where I have arranged to meet William for lunch. The store sells goods that you would find in any such store in the west but at prices so far beyond the pockets of most Chinese people one wonders how it survives commercially. In the basement is a huge supermarket and at street-level is one of *Weifang's* three fast food restaurants – a branch of KFC.

William arrives and we take the lift to the top floor which is given over to a selection of different types of restaurant. It is a pleasure to have someone interpret the menu and help make a choice of dish. Like most young Chinese men William has had few choices in life. His parents are peasant workers from *JieYuan* village in *Shanxi* province and wanting the best for him encouraged his academic progress through school. He has a younger brother and a sister who is at teacher-training college. Because of his parents' working pattern he was always close to his grandmother. Now he lives in *Weifang* which is a twenty hour train journey away from his home and, given his financial situation, a place he will visit only once a year. He receives a small government loan but otherwise has to survive on whatever his parents can send or what he can earn himself. Once he has paid for his tuition and dormitory fees there is little left for other expenses such as food or clothes. The university canteen is cheap and he might get by on 14 yuan - £1.00 - a day. If he can persuade someone to take him on as an English teacher he might be able to earn 30 yuan an hour. There is not much fat on William.

In common with everyone who has any contact with English or foreigners his name is both a way of embracing the language and also an acknowledgement of the difficulty of pronouncing his Chinese name. Sometimes the name comes from the *meaning* of a Chinese name and sometimes directly from the *sound* of a Chinese name: if you play with his name – *Huibin* – you can just about hear the English – *William*. The sound of words is an important cultural feature. For instance the number "four" is deemed unlucky because the word for it - *sur* – is similar to the word for death.

At the university he lives with another seven young men in a dormitory, as do school children and many workers too. The four bunk beds are arranged around the walls with just enough room in the middle for a table. A balcony leads on to toilet facilities and provides a drying space for clothes. One of the students has brought his own computer here and downloading concerts from the flavour of the month pop group Westlife seems to be a popular pastime. No females are allowed in these dormitories and neither is alcohol. The power is cut at eleven every evening when the building is locked. Recreational drugs are unknown and alcohol is rarely taken and this is confirmed as the meal progresses and his low tolerance to the beer we have ordered manifests itself in a slowing of his speech.

Somewhere in the region of fifty percent of young people go to university: as with most countries there are sought-after universities – here it is Beijing and Shanghai – and the others. With moderate grades at school William had to make a choice and *Weifang* was chosen because of its fame as the kite capital of the world. Although it has a history of over fifty years the campus is modern with all of the facilities one would expect. There is a small lake, fountains, woodland – not a bad place to be on the eastern side of the city. With over a hundred students in classes learning is a matter of personal motivation and last year he was lucky because one of the English tutors spent time with him and his friends. Many Chinese are desperate for this sort of contact so they can improve their spoken English – hence our own meeting. He is a very well balanced person who understands the way life is dealing with him and exhibits the "can-do" mentality that is found everywhere here.

In a sense his progress is the progress of the country; grandparents and parents would not have dreamed of university or such mobility. His country roots would have been devoid of comforts. I notice a scar on his arm. He tells me the story of when he was young. He was playing on the *kang* – the heated brick bed found in country dwellings. It was next to the cooking pan – a large bowl set into the range – and he fell in. His aunt whipped him out but the burn has left him scarred. If he succeeds at university he might get a job which will pay enough for an apartment in the city with bathroom and kitchen and maybe a motorbike or even a car. This is the progress of China: from poverty to wealth; from country to city; from ignorance to education.

Unfortunately, the sheer numbers of graduates ensures that there are not enough jobs to go round and that wages are depressed. I have met many university graduates who are working in shops or in hotels. To get into more suitable positions they need to be able to exercise *guangxi* – the system of connections that gets you preferment because of who you know, not what you know. Even then, working conditions can be unimaginably weighted against the employee. There are stories of workers having to put down a deposit of a year's salary to ensure that they do not leave. There are stories of workers receiving only a portion of their salary if the boss decides not to pay fully. Workers have to work long days and have few holidays. For a worker living in dormitories there must be little privacy. William hopes that he will secure a post as a tour guide; for this

28

his English will have to be good and he will need the knowledge and skills to communicate information. The only time that I see him angry and dispirited is when he has been bumped off the list of student volunteers who have been assigned as translators to the visiting foreigners at the Kite Festival.

As our relationship develops I find there is no problem with his grasp of history or literature as he regales me with ancient stories in *Suzhou*, or provides insights into history in Shanghai. In return he is delighted to travel to places which have such importance in the culture of China. In a small way his horizons are expanded when I offer him his first taste of coffee or a meal in a tapas bar. For the first time, in this western setting and having to wield a knife and fork rather than chopsticks, he gets an impression, with the unfamiliar architecture and high density of foreigners, of what it is like to be travelling in a strange place.

One item on the cultural life-map that is also beginning to change, albeit slowly, is the concept of marriage. A first generation urban dweller such as William is likely to adhere to the traditional scheme of things. Between twenty-three and thirty a wife will be found by him, his parents, or a matchmaker. There will be a child, preferably a boy – or children if he can afford the fine, or lives in the country. He and his wife will work hard and his parents will dote on the child; if they all live together they will be the principal carers and will bring it up, as China is recognising, to be a spoilt "little emperor." Urban sophisticates may not keep to this tradition. A class of well-educated and financially independent young women is more likely to call the tune, especially as there is a shortage of eligible brides due to the one-child policy. This stabilised the population but was responsible for the disposal of girl babies to orphanages or adoption abroad or, sadly, by infanticide. Ironically, in villages now, girls of marriageable age command a high price and are even kidnapped and forcibly married. Otherwise young men have no alternative but to drift to the cities where the choice is a little wider. On the other hand one thirty-year old male that I met, Scott, was suffering from a very real dilemma. His parents, keenly aware that he is reaching the outer bounds of marriageability, have presented him with a succession of young women. His lack of interest in them and his greater interest for continuing education have meant that the young women will find someone else and his parents remain without an heir. Scott is constantly agonising over his duty to his parents on the one hand and his desire for further qualifications on the other.

For William this is in the future. For now his concerns are those of a student. Scraping together enough money to live and study, passing exams and getting a job. His boundless good nature and optimism will carry him far.

CITYSCAPE

Did you or your children enjoy playing with Lego? If you or they did and enjoyed the outcomes then you would feel at home here. Anything built within the last twenty years or so reflects the LEGO approach to architecture. Squares, triangles, rectangles, spires, circles, diamonds, curves - all feature prominently. Anything that can be done with steel, concrete and glass is. The effect is enhanced by the sheer bulk of most projects and seeming lack of any guiding principle and certainly not the golden mean. To complete that "LEGO" feel buildings are clad in ceramic tiles of white or bold primary colours or sometimes mosaic patterns which reflect harshly the sunlight or glisten in the rain. It is like being in a giant public urinal. As a nod in the direction of tradition there will sometimes be a curved-up roof somewhere on the building. All large cityscapes feature many high-rise buildings so that in many ways they have an international flavour which will shock the traveller from the west who may have been expecting something more traditional.

Such buildings have evolved over the last twenty-five years. The preceding years saw the erection of four/six storey floor blocks of apartments brown and flat-roofed, built in the soviet style and now being demolished to make way for more LEGO. Below these and sometimes in little enclaves of their own are alleyways of single story dwellings, sometimes with a garden, courtyard or compound. Roughly built of brick with a pitched roof they must have been the housing that town and city dwellers used for centuries and they bear a resemblance to the compound houses that are to be found in the countryside. Enter the covered double gateway and you are faced with a wall, sometimes with a ceramic mural on it. This is to confuse the bad spirits who like to travel in straight lines. The courtyard is lined with buildings which serve a number of functions.

Buildings here are either no older than about forty years or not less than two thousand years. That is an overstatement of course but the ancient buildings that there are reflect an incredibly staid line of tradition. Think about Europe and even a novice observer could name half a dozen periods of architectural significance. Here it is one – and you will have seen it. Curved-up roofs, with ceramic tiles, finials in the shapes of dragons, formal doorways, symmetry, stairways, courtyards. Furthermore, all buildings of quality look similar whatever their function whether they are a temple, tomb or palace. They are aligned on a N/S axis facing South with the principal apartment approached through a series of ever grander gateways. Rooms generally do not interconnect but open onto the courtyard. The reason for this was partly due to the stasis that comes from China being isolated from innovative ideas from other parts of the globe and partly from the inherent and enormously powerful influence of tradition from succeeding dynasties.

What happened forty years ago of course was the Cultural Revolution which attempted to remove all traces of this dynastic past and indeed swept away many old structures whatever their beauty or historical significance – no actually *because* of those features! The replacement utilitarian structures were celebrated for their purposeful undecadent dullness. Cities across the country have piles of these soviet-style blocks, many without sanitary facilities. In any event, buildings of fifty years old, or sometimes younger, are knocked down to make way for the latest development and there is a seething construction glut with a cycle of dilapidation, clearance and building happening everywhere all of the time with many sites worked 24 hours a day. It is no wonder the air is often laden with dust and grit. The legacy from this seems to be an attitude which prioritises new-build and ignores maintenance, so that buildings on the way up will be next to buildings on the way down.

In terms of city planning there is a rigid N/S grid pattern with wide roads although even in the middle of the city a road might sometimes degenerate into pothole decay or outright mud track and sewer. Trees are planted liberally along large and small roads. There are many parks, sometimes arranged around water, and other open spaces. The housing developments themselves are relatively dull lego-build in serried ranks in gated communities with maybe sculpted roofs and a sculpture or ornamental rock at the entrance.

Villages are also arranged on a grid pattern with few metalled roads. As windows tend to face onto the inner courtyard the wayfarer is faced with a series of blind walls pierced by gateways only. The effect is unhappily one of monotony as there is none of the joy of finding buildings from different periods, sizes or styles. Although an amazing 60% of the population still lives in the country the trend is to move to the city. Those who make big money in the city live there – there is no modern tradition of having a country estate. For the few who make it to the top there are housing developments of individual dwellings mostly built in a sort of faux French colonial style. People generally tend to live where they work so there is mercifully no history yet of the commuter.

Time to get out the lego . . .

It is difficult to love the land of *Shandong* Province. It is occupied by worn-out, shabby cities and overused land. It is true that in the west there are pleasant hills and mountains, but in the east the plains are featureless and never-ending the only elevated spots composed of rubbish and rubble. Often referred to as China's breadbasket the cost of this is the industrial zeal with which the land has been plundered. Every inch is cultivated to yield some sort of crop so the landscape everywhere is the subject of rigid organisation. Streams are carried in aqueducts, trees are planted in rows, banks of polytunnels face precisely south. Anything random has been eradicated. In ancient times it was different and the Yellow River ranged randomly across this plain so that the inhabitants could never quite be sure of its path. The pay-off for having to keep moving home was the fertile alluvial soil, some of it conveyed from the high Tibetan plateau, that was left behind. At one time the river's variable route carried it south into the Yellow Sea, but now it enters the *Bohai* Gulf some two hundred kilometres to the north.

Taking the bus north across this wasted landscape in the November sun the middens and heaps of rubbish are still there and the towns are still nondescript but familiarity is beginning to strip away the alien feel of the place. The dust and waterless riverbeds are softened by a haze. It is easier to imagine that one is part of the country rather than a traveller viewing things through foreign eyes. Eventually the road hits the coast of the *Shandong* peninsular and *Penglai* appears. My well-rehearsed Mandarin secures me a room.

After the noise and bustle of *Weifang* this is a pleasant place to be. I have done my homework and found out about the place from the internet which revealed:

"pengai is knwon as china's 'home of myth',qin emperor's seeking prescription ,han emperor's visiting fairy ,the great poets bai yu yi and su dong po's verses,fairy tale of "eight immotals crassing the sea" and wonder of mirage ,all portray a mysterious fairy world which make penple yearn for."

This sort of nonsense is found everywhere and one develops a knack of getting the idea; my own limited Mandarin renders me a bit of a hypocrite in this but one would think that more care would be taken over publicly available text. The attraction here is the *Penglai* Pavilion which is a collection of buildings on a headland combined with an ancient harbour which at one time was China's naval dockyard. The harbour is silted up and is being reclaimed but boat skeletons found there are proudly displayed along with excellent models of all sorts of watercraft. The buildings, however, are temples with lurid evocations of Buddha. The temples are set amongst the rocks and boulders in courtyards with ancient trees and incense burners. There is a fine curtain wall that sweeps up the cliff to a lighthouse like tower. Despite a chill morning mist it is pleasant to wander in and out of the complex.

Almost all Chinese people know the myth of "Eight Immortals Crossing the Sea" which is said to have originated here. According to the myth, the Eight Immortals, after having been drinking at the *Penglai* Pavilion, crossed the sea, not in a boat but through their supernatural powers, and finally reached Japan. A giant sculpture of the heavenly octet faces one on the sea front and pictures of them are everywhere in *Penglai*. The reference to drink is important here as a catalyst to their supernatural journey. The spirit of choice is *baijiu* distilled from grain and utterly undrinkable. Once, at the end of a wedding reception, I watched a waitress cleaning tables with it – apparently there is nothing to match it. Rather mischievously the direct translation of *baijiu* is *white spirit*! Business meals and family banquets are organised around consumption of this evil liquid. To show friendship one must drain one's glass if someone proposes a toast to you – anything less dishonours the proposer. To accrue "face" or credibility one must drink a quantity of the stuff. At a banquet one's glass is replenished as soon as the last toast is over and with a cry of *gambai* the next toast is proposed and the contents are flung back. Because personal development is so often advanced at these drinking sessions there is almost certainly a high correlation between hard drinkers and captains of industry. There is probably too a correlation between hard drinkers and the sort of supernatural powers that they assume – enough to carry them over the ocean.

The other story that draws people here is the *Penglai* Mirage. Every so often a vision appears out at sea which is sometimes a hazy blur but on good days can develop into an image of a town complete with buildings, cars and people moving about. One sighting in the past was fortuitously recorded on film and for a few yuan you can watch the forty-minute show. As if to milk the maximum tourist potential from the site a new development on the next headland includes a 360 degree cinema, museum, a tower and park reached by a cableway which takes a short cut across the bay. There is also a "plank walk" cantilevered from the cliff which leads to a monument marking the notional division between the *Bohai* and Yellow Seas. It is all harmless and it is good to watch the sea and the ferries churning over the waves to the islands that are just out of view.

The following day is brighter and I explore a bit of the town which leads me to the old fishing area. The houses are in good condition and bear evidence of their trade. Nets are hanging, buoys and weights and ropes are strung around. In parts of the street small fish are drying on the road. A narrow lane emerges on the sea front. In front of me a grand structure has been built out into the sea which consists of two gigantic circular enclosures. The nearer and larger is a seal pool with a large teahouse in the middle. The smaller pool has a pagoda in the centre. The path that encompasses both of them is lined with grotesquely shaped rocks that have been labelled according to whatever they resemble: camel, crawling baby and so on. It occurs to me that this is a Tourist Attraction.

I settle down to watch the scene. Parents and children play on the sand. Fishermen in high waders are casting out almost up to their armpits in the water. High bowed fishing boats are dotted all over the sea at rest. The breeze is fresh but warm. Four kilometres to the west the distinctive wall and tower of the pavilion rise up out of the sea. A man is sitting immobile on the sea wall for a long time looking out to sea. Maybe he is watching out for the next mirage, or maybe he is getting over a night with too much *baijiu*.

What is the difference between *Shandong* Province in China and Spain? At the moment about twenty degrees and Spain is where I should be! It was the first weekend in December and I had just come back from cycling out to the South East of the city in pursuit of what looked on the map to be a delightful elevated spot – possibly the hill from which kites are flown in the Spring Festival. When I got there the large grassy mound that might have been there last year had been scooped out to some depth, a pipe flowed into stagnant water at the bottom and new housing was being erected all around.

As I turned to go home I was keenly aware that the wind that had been flowing with me at my speed was now cruelly and coldly against me. Hurling myself into the biting wind I set my mind to the 7 or 8 kilometers that lay ahead along the noisome roads trying to find routes that would offer shelter but with little luck.

Just as I found my way indoors the damp chill that I had been battling with precipitated into flurries of snow and from that moment onwards the temperature here has plummeted reaching   -16 degrees on some nights. Unlike other first-timers to China, I had heeded the received wisdom of the community and bought a set of underwear – a top and long johns and mightily pleased to be able to put them on in future sorties outside.

The school has a central heating system which operates at its peak at 6.30am, 12.00 and 8.00pm but has to be supplemented at other times in my apartment by a wall mounted hot-air blower. I swear that my apartment is in a different microclimate from the rest of the school. Walking from class into the area under an arch, one is assailed by a darkening and a cold whirling which must drop the temperature a couple of degrees at least. It is therefore almost a pleasure to go and teach in the school buildings and feel the sun.

This is where you would stop recognizing the place as a school. The rooms where I teach are arranged end to end around a quadrangle on three tiers. Access is from an open walkway or balcony on each level. Thus each room has windows (ill-fitting) and whatever elements there currently are on two sides. Two radiators perform weakly. The children do their classes portly with underwear and several layers of clothing, scarves and hats – as does the staff. Despite the skin-cringing cold, doors and windows are often left open and children are delighted to rush out for the ten minute breaks which interleave the lessons. There is a belief that boiling vinegar and garlic in the room will dispel any bugs around so I often find I'm teaching in a chemical haze that reminds me of making chutney – and having to hop over the pan of boiling vinegar.

Now compare that picture with the cossetedness of our centrally-heated culture which shuts down whenever the temperature gets into "Offices and Factories Act" territory and children complain of the cold – but only when they're not complaining of the heat. Especially consider that many people expect the heat to come from somewhere external to themselves rather than their own body's generated or conserved heat. When I go for a walk I am amazed to see stallholders still on the streets or groups of men sitting playing mah jong in this windy coldness. Cyclists still ply the roads. You rarely see anyone visibly hunched against the cold or hurrying to get out of the wind.

If I am sounding gung-ho about all this believe me I am not as I hate this level of cold and endure it as best as I can. I had been asked to go to a school on the outskirts of the city on Sunday – with the customary minimum of information. Meeting my host at 8.30 on this arctic morning was not my idea of a rest but I put on a brave face – and several layers - and found the school new (and warm) in the farmed area to the North of the expressway. The children were responsive and – as ever – very friendly. I taught three classes of these country children Old Macdonald and got so warm that layers began to peel off. Thankfully my host warned me to prepare for the shock of re-emerging into the frozen waste or I'd probably have had to be chipped off the steps. On the way back the usual questions from my host – How old was I? How much was my salary? – but he knew all about the city and was able to tell me where the kite-flying hill – called FuyuanShan - was. Another cycle journey to plan. But maybe in the spring when it's warmer.

Officially a secular society, China believes only in the guiding hand of the communist party. The big holiday in October is National Golden Day and then, of course, Chinese New Year in January. Buddhism and Taoism have their place but do not give rise to any official feast days. Nevertheless all shops from the most decadent department stores to the humblest restaurant have been sporting Christmas imagery for the last month. Snow scenes, cheerful Father Christmas cut-outs, Christmas trees, and all the paraphernalia that clutters the West. The locals are not stupid and see this imposed festival as merely a marketing opportunity, but they are also happy enough to have another holiday to relieve the long hours that they work. It has only been in evidence for about half a dozen years, but long enough for small children to confuse Santa Claus with Confucius.

However, an earnest fifteen-year old stated quite strongly to me that she felt that China should be sticking to its own traditions and should not be importing ready-made ones from elsewhere. She is quite right of course. The joy of visiting other people whether they are in the next village or a country half-way around the world is their difference. Weifang already has MacDonald's, KFC and Wal-Mart – and now Christmas. It is one thing to observe one community's Divali or another's Hanukah out of interest and quite another to adopt a feast day as one's own, especially as there are absolutely no religious or cultural links. Agreed, in the west Christmas also seems to be a commercial event that has now been fractured by the godless from its religious roots, but at least in Europe and the USA the celebration has a long history.

So how does *Weifang* celebrate Christmas? On Wednesday 21 the city hosted a massive corporate function at the *Fu Hua* Hotel, a palace of crystal, chrome and gilt. Potential investors in the city were invited and the foreigners were there almost certainly to impress them; white faces carry a lot of kudos. The food and entertainment was good.

On Friday 23 the school has classroom parties for all of the children in the evening. There is a convivial, relaxed atmosphere as the children perform songs and jokes to each other. On the following day the school management take foreign staff for a lunchtime banquet.

On Sunday – Christmas day itself I go with a couple of English colleagues to *DongYuan* Park where we meet with Chinese friends. It is cold, the ice is frozen but the sun is bright. We serve them with a cake specially commissioned, a triumph of cream and calligraphy. They in turn treat us to lunch at a restaurant. The food is abundant the wine flows and we all have to participate in the karaoke. In the evening at another party with ex. pats. I count seven nationalities. It breaks up early next morning. I have to teach in a few hours time!

On Saturday 30 snow has fallen, the bronze busts on the school drive now have whitened pates; there is a party for the staff who are all expected to do a turn. Most of the Chinese staff respond with karaoke. The foreign staff sing a song from the Czech Republic. For this we have practiced for a week with Daria who has taught us not only the tune but also the awkwardCzech pronunciation also. The kitchen provides a good lunch. That evening there is a New Year's party in the Kiss Bar, a favourite with ex.pats. I learn incidentally that Monday 2 is a non-teaching day. I also learnt incidentally this week that my holiday could start a week earlier on the 7th so I fly out of Weifang for five weeks. I have worked all the way through Christmas and the New Year. In China the long spring holiday starts in January and ends in February.

SPRING HOLIDAY

"*Feiji zhan*" I said to the driver in my best mandarin. When he looked blankly the second and third time I resorted to pantomiming an aeroplane and showing him my flight tickets. Light dawned. "Ah" he said "*feiji zhan*" but with that infinitesimal difference of tone which changes it from meaning "may I paint the goulash of your wife's sister?" to "airport."

A four hour flight brings me to Guangzhou (Gwang-joe) an important business city the size of London in the south west of China where the language is not mandarin but canton. The reservation service in the airport tells me it will cost 200 yuan to get to my hotel, then when I look disbelieving 150: business obviously starts at the airport! A tout tells me 180 Yuan, then 120, but caves in when I walk off after telling him 100. The car I find myself in is unmarked and when the driver starts talking about picking up a "friend" I get worried; I am carrying all my holiday money in cash. After the third time around the airport I knew this was not for me. I begin to have visions of being cornered in a dark street and wondering if I could snatch the keys from the ignition to disable the car. As the car draws into "airport arrivals" yet again I leap out and into a legitimate taxi. "*Shamian Binguan*" I say to the driver and he understands at once. So that's where I had been going wrong – I had been speaking canton instead of mandarin! The airport expressway carves its way through the town mostly at 2nd or 3rd floor level, brusquely knocking corners off buildings or cruising past dining rooms and neon signs and lands me in a lovely oasis. The cost - 92 yuan. I think I won that round.

Shamian Island used to be a colonial enclave for the European commissions doing trade with China and still retains elegant classical buildings fronting the Pearl

River. This could be Paris 1920. Ancient trees with aerial roots, graceful parks, colonnades and wide boulevards place it in a time capsule. I realized I had been in China too long when instead of being an object of interest to the natives I myself was turning to stare every time I heard an American accent. English is the dominant language on signs and there are restaurants with names like "Lucy's Bar." There seems to be a high security presence. Not only are there are a couple of embassies on the island but The White Swan Hotel is a favourite with foreigners who come to adopt surplus Chinese babies – the sad plight of dumped female children who are the unforeseen consequence of China's "one child" policy.

The island is separated from the rest of *Guangzhou* by a small channel and stepping over the bridges onto the mainland is like moving into another country. Imagine the peace and solitude of covering your eyes and ears and then opening them/closing/opening; the effect of stepping on or off those bridges was similar. On one side - traffic, harsh lighting, people, small shops, street hawkers, fish markets, more people, pavement cafes, building sites, gaudy hoardings, grimy buildings – on the other serene avenues, ordered and well-maintained mansions, green spaces, a few youths playing in the parks, bronze statues carefully illuminated.

One of the places that you can escape from the mayhem of Guangzhou's streets apart from *Shamian Island* is *BaiyunShan*. This is an enormous landscaped mountain area in the north of the city. The Chinese do these things well and *Baiyun* is no exception. A lot of the area is given over to the native forest, but roads and paths discreetly placed give access to the peaks or provide contour hugging tracks that give maximum views with minimum effort. There are feature gardens and areas for which you pay extra but otherwise the whole lot is a mere 5 yuan admission. Given the climate, which is sup-tropical, palms and other exotica give the place a holiday feel. Lakeside restaurants and pavilions on the summits are part of the traditional garden plan.

However, *Guangzhou* is not really on my itinerary; it is merely a convenient transport hub between *Weifang* and Hong Kong and I am impatient to be out of this large and impersonal city. I locate not only a ferry operator but also a hotel willing to get me to the port. I am on my way.

Emerging from the metro on that warm winter evening it was already dark and I was immediately faced with a perceptual overload. A blizzard of sound and light – cars, shop-windows hoardings and people. *Causeway* is on Hong Kong Island and is the principal shopping, entertainment and eating area; wherever you look there were hoards of people moving en masse. After months of functional illiteracy in a Chinese-only world I was also taking in mountains of print information from the signs and advertisements. Maybe I was picking up vibrations from the hundreds of people around me, or maybe the kilometers of neon on the buildings were inducing some sort of "upper" but I was definitely picking up the buzz that large and exciting cities seem to possess. I was alert and ready to do anything.

That week I rode buses, escalators, trams, trains, ferries & a junk; I saw films and concerts; I visited galleries, exhibitions and museums; I ate Thai, Chinese, French, Italian, Organic; I looked at ancient temples in vernacular buildings and tower blocks designed by the finest world architects; I wandered through ageless street-markets and 21st century shopping malls. The air of optimism is infectious, there is such visible prosperity and the whole place is so spick and span and efficient that one feels enjoined to share in the delights; this is a "can-do" culture – and I did!

You don't have to spend much time here before you start to wonder why everywhere cannot be run like this, a truly civilized society, elegant buildings, well-fed and happy citizens, a plethora of choice. Take transport: I decided to visit some museums before going to an evening concert; this entailed 13 changes throughout the day and all were managed with a minimum of trouble. All of the transport options – tram, bus, over and under-ground rail and ferry – all are integrated, join up with each other and use a unified payment system. I defy anyone to cite such a journey in any other city on earth; I feel accomplished if I manage three or four changes on the London underground. On the spot fines are used to ensure a litter-free city. The parks are beautifully kept. At this point I have to burst the bubble slightly by mentioning that in some parts of the region population density at over 50,000 per square kilometer is the highest in the world and that Hong Kong Inc. is kept afloat by thousands of low-paid Filipinos who nevertheless are better-off here than they would be at home.

The Hong Kong cityscape is iconic; in case you have forgotten it is an island which faces the mainland area of Kowloon across a busy strait. Both sides sport immense skyscrapers designed by people from the Who's Who of Architecture. As if this is not enough the buildings have a wonderful green backdrop of peaks which rise as high as 300 metres. At eight every night there is a light show using video, neon, laser and moving theatre lanterns where orchestrated illumination plays on all of the surfaces – hard, curved, reflective – to bring out the sculptural forms. Watching this from a harbour side bar is a delight. Without any regret at all I can see why, in recent colonial times, it was described as the jewel in the crown.

But what I fail to understand is why no one ever told me about the immense unpopulated areas that exist to the north of Kowloon and its suburbs in the New Territories. One of these areas – the Sai Kung Peninsula – was the object of my travels for a day. Trails – sometime hard-going - across this wilderness take in sub-tropical valleys and peaks with fantastic views of inlets, lakes, forests, and small towns in the distance. For the whole day I passed only one other walker, a real anti-dote to the frenetic pace of the city. The walk finished with a relatively easy path which followed the shore. At one point I became curious about the large "birds" that seemed to be noisily disturbing the foliage and found that they were – wild monkeys! With similar but less grand topography, Lamma Island thirty minutes to the south of Hong Kong offers a different beauty; sandy beaches, cheap accommodation in the palm studded folds of the low hills, seaside restaurants, and car-less paths. Even on the largely settled area of Hong Kong Island there are many trails around the peaks or through the valleys.

Macau, just an hour away by fast ferry on the west side of the river mouth, is a Portuguese ex-colony, but much more like mainland China than Hong Kong. Indeed, after the electric efficiency of its neighbour it is a bit of a culture shock. Life is slower, the bus-drivers less helpful, everything is a little more effort – like finding a bar that will serve you on a Sunday lunchtime. It is treated as a playground for Chinese gamblers who have a half-dozen or so casinos to choose from. With intentional irony I would say that these casinos are a re-run of Las Vegas

– but without the charisma. Loud, glittery, neon-clad elephantine structures, frocked with redundant ironmongery; the competition must have been to design the ugliest building – and the Hotel Lisboa wins!

These are all on the Eastern side of the peninsula: on the Western side with a little ferreting one can still find some magnificent remnants from the colonial past mixed in with the more earthy high-density housing. By the side of one pleasant park and colonial mansion lies a chapel and cemetery devoted to British citizens; a strange and affecting reminder of a time when this foreign territory in pre-aviation days was a home, made more distant by the rigours of sea travel. Many of them were in the navy (including a Churchill) and in the harbour area, which must be little changed from these times, you can still find small shipwrights with industrial size presses next to bakers or restaurants, chandlers, sailor's hostels from a century ago, a fireworks factory, or - to complete the seedy port scene – bevies of ladies offering to give you a "massage-e."

Due south of the peninsula are two islands, Taipa and Coloane connected by bridges and causeways to each other which are less populated and which also have some well-preserved areas where villas, churches, plazas, and streets seem to be straight out of The Algarve. Curious this – travelling long and hard from the UK, and then enthusing over the sort of place that you could have seen after a short hop across the channel! The charm of Coloane village, strung out along the coast lies in its unusually good state of preservation mixed with the evidence that it is still a working community. Fish are strung out to dry, nets are being mended, dwellings start on the street and extend out over the sea on a crazy network of piers. There is not a single souvenir shop and the nearest sops to tourism are the restaurants – which would probably be there anyway. An Englishman, an expharmacist here for 26 years, runs the excellent Lord Stowe's bakery which not only produces an interesting variety of his own dishes, but also the delicious local speciality: small custard tarts.

The small but stylish airport departures lounge featured a live band. A nice parting gesture as you would expect Macau to want to woo "arrivals," rather than those who have already spent their money there.

Travelling is not all delights and joys. Waking up in *Xiamen* (Siar-men) on the fifteenth floor of yet another hotel there's that feeling of ennui that comes from the need to acquaint oneself with yet another set of bus destinations and get the lie of another city. The airport reservation service had warned against my hotel choice – it was old and was poorly situated they said but at that time of night I had pressed ahead anyway. In the daylight I now peered down from my room on a construction site and a busy road intersection which was only slightly allayed by some forested hills behind the railway station. A look at my map confirmed that I had confused east and west *Hubin* road and was about 6km from the seafront. Breakfast on the third floor was no better. Service was helpful but the place was depressing.

Resolved to change I checked-out, took a taxi to the seafront and across the water to the island of *Gulangyue*

(Gwal-ang-yew) and took my time choosing a hotel near the harbour. This island is filled with the mansions from a hundred years of European trade missions and their consulates now all departed. The streets are a happy tangle of paths negotiating the hills on the southern end of the island. You can walk around it in a couple of hours. The buildings are western and the vegetation is tropical – the perfect mix. It has no high risers and no cars. Just what I needed.

Services are limited and I have to find my own laundry but the roads seem to have no logic – a street name sometimes applies to roads that extend in three directions or double back on themselves. No matter as on the way I encounter a memorial hall and garden celebrating a midwife reputed to have delivered 50,000 children, and a PIANO museum set in cliff-top house. Amongst the Pleyels, Steinways and player pianos was a real curiosity - a corner piano with its 90 degree keyboards dovetailing into each other. *Gualangyue* is famed for its music. It has its own music school, concert hall and the museum ensures that with a population of 18,000 there is a greater density of pianos per capita than anywhere else on earth!

On the mainland I visit an attractive temple which is built into a rocky hillside and which segued into an enormous botanical garden which ranged over several hundred acres and included a substantial cactus house. However, I find these desultory delights and the chill drizzly weather do not come up to my expectations of *Xiamen*. It had been pegged as an interesting place by more than one source and the temperature charts promised a warm climate in January. In fact it is merely another city and I have seen these streets and these markets before in other cities. Not only do I cut short my stay here but I also change my next destination. After another one of those humbling experiences where a member of the public devotes an hour of her time to helping me secure the necessary flight change with no thought of reward, I secure a ticket for *Lijiang*.

In the totally glass-fronted room my early-morning field of view was completely filled by a granite wall a kilometer away, 1000m up to the ridge and 1000m down to the *Yangzi* (Yang-tsur) powering its way through the gorge. I had arrived at Sean's Guest House the day before yesterday after an early morning start from *Lijiang* (Lee-jang). My Chinese companion, Leo, and I had caught the rattletrap local bus to *Daju* (Dar-jew) at 8.00 in the morning which had trundled round every part of the town to pick up passengers and goods before leaving for the road into the mountains. I was glad that the driver, for once, was careful on the winding precipitous roads which snaked up and down the passes. The last twenty km. was unpaved. At the road's end we lunched on vegetables and rice at a courtyard house before descending the steep dusty track to the fast-flowing *Yangzi* where a boatman, in his own time, ferried us across. This is the same *Yangzi* which has risen in high Tibet to the North, floats giant pleasure boats through the three gorges and makes its exodus to the sea in Shanghai. At 6,400km it is the third longest river in the world. Here it was 50m across, deep and very fast.

A scramble up the bank opposite, then back on ourselves across cultivated land overlooking *Daju* and then through a village landed us on a road above the gorge facing upstream. Although uphill and in the sun the going was relatively easy apart from the fierce headwind. At one point Leo decided to make a detour to see the river already now a long way below the road and thus began the mystery which I have never resolved. Having discussed where we might spend the night there was a tacit assumption in my mind at least that he would catch up with me at Sean's in the village called Walnut Garden where I arrived ninety minutes later.

Sean's is more of an institution than a guesthouse. On the backpacker's trail it was populated with thirty or so Europeans sitting on the terrace at stone tables overlooking the gorge swapping tales and information which I soon joined in with; so congenial was the company and the food and so glorious the surroundings that I decided to spend an extra night there. By the time I went to bed Leo had not appeared.

The following day he did not appear. It was a loose arrangement that we had made so I assumed that he had decided to go on alone and passed by when I had not been looking. A decision had to be made though. Should I continue on the road to *Qiatou* (Sha-to) or attempt the climb up to the more interesting mountain track. Bear in mind that I was now alone, not good with heights and did not fancy battling with the headwind that continued to race down the valley. I did my research and all of the walkers, who seemed to be walking in the opposite direction extolled the virtues of the latter offering useful tips on the awkward parts.

On that second morning when I awoke I checked the movement of the trees and there was no wind so the high road it was. Once I was on the track 2km from Sean's the ascent, the morning cold and the concern that I may be doing something foolhardy induced a panicky shortage of breath. However – mad dogs and Englishmen . . !

I regained my composure about half way up where the track emerged out of the shadow cast by the mountain on the other side of the gorge-at eleven o'clock. Climbing through spindly pine and scrub above a waterfall the rational part of me reflected that hundreds of people followed this path all the time, local children and old people included. Nevertheless, at one point discretion got the better of me where the path was badly worn and I sidled across close to the rock face, only to find that this was the highest point – 2,800m – and bumped into a couple of students I had been trailing.

What can I say of the views? The spires of five-finger mountain, the play of sunlight on the outcrops of rock, the villages with terraced fields above and below, the sheer waterfalls, the track pacing away on its ledge, the village of Daju disappearing on its plain behind, and below, 2,000m below, the white water of an angry youthful *Yangzi*. The story goes that when tigers still inhabited this region one of them evaded capture from a band of hunters by leaping across the gorge using a rock in the middle as a stepping stone. My fellow walkers pointed out the fabled rock far below.

The track at about 2,500m is sometimes on narrow ledges above sheer drops and sometimes passing through villages where the incline allowed terracing. At these points appeared the guesthouses and that evening I stayed at the Teahorse guesthouse opposite Snow Mountain, a magnificent bare massif topped with snow. A couple of French youths were there and we spent the cold evening in the owner's kitchen huddled around the stove swapping silly finger puzzles with her teenage children.

The third day of walking and I felt much more relaxed although the morning chill still took my breath away. At ten o'clock the sun was still not to be seen; the sky was clear with a sliver of moon to the south. Soon, however,

52

the sharp peaks of Snow Mountain were framed with rays of light jetting upwards and around like a halo in a renaissance painting. I stopped and stared. Without any further prelude the sun came spilling over the summit; within thirty seconds it came from nothing to everything. The effect was palpable; it was not just the heat; it was as if an elemental force was acting on you.

Pine trees around me with butterflies, eagles above, a good path underfoot and slanting sunlight across the gorge. Villagers that I passed had their arms in great bloody vats of meat and offal and were filling membranes to make sausages for the forthcoming Chinese New Year celebrations. On one verandah next to a satellite dish a dead pig lay on a bench, on another a live pig was tethered to a tree in readiness.

The last climb took me through a bamboo forest whose whisperings were yet drowned by the river below and it was with a sense of regret that I then started on the descent as the gorge opened out into a broader valley. While the sound of birds and river roar gave way to traffic noise I considered how privileged I was to have walked this trail in this way. It will not stay wild and beautiful for much longer. I am sure that organized tours, quacking guides with megaphones and flags, will soon be climbing purpose-made steps or riding a cableway. Worse still are the proposals to dam and flood the valley just as has been done with the *Yangzi*'s more mature incarnation further downstream. A paved road has already been constructed no doubt to facilitate these developments. The sense of wilderness will vanish, a tamer gorge.

I survived it too of course so there was a sense of achievement. This is not to be melodramatic for every year the gorge claims lives. At the very time that I had been walking a German called Peter was lost for days. He had taken a high path and spent two nights on the mountain without shelter, food or water before finding a way down. Another English walker, Marcus, found himself on the wrong side of a scree slope and feared for his life as it gave way beneath him. He showed me the cuts and bruises. And then of course I never did find out what happened to Leo.

Biking north from *Lijiang* (Lee-jang) along the wide flat valley towards Jade Dragon Snow Mountain I passed through many villages where the inhabitants were busy preparing for that evening's New Year feast. Women were washing vegetables in the water that rushed down the stone channels that bordered the paved roads and men were sellotaping red and gold scripts over the gateways that were intended to bring luck for the next year. The Chinese Year of the Dog was almost upon us.

Unlike the other villages, *Baisha* (By-shar) had a gate at its southern entrance and a few shops aimed at tourists – batik & ceramics mostly. Set behind a few trees Dr. Ho's house was not to be missed with framed newspaper cuttings outside from the world's press. He invited me in – as he does with everyone that visits the village and immediately launched into a description of his life history supplementing it with copious documents. He also gave me a cup of his healthy tea.

Born in 1923 he studied western medicine at *Nanjing* University but his forte is herbal preparations, the knowledge for these coming from his own father. He, his son and hopefully his student grandson continue the tradition. He collects the herbs – 600 of them – from the slopes of nearby Snow Mountain, dries and mixes them to treat diabetes, cancer, stomach problems, anything.

54

He took me through the case history of a patient with a tumour who had come to him, conventional medicine having failed. He showed me the copies of official hospital diagnoses before and after; they spoke for themselves. He claims many other successes and showed me letters requesting his preparations from all over the world including one from a former British ambassador. He is known internationally and has traveled to the USA to present his knowledge. He also receives many visitors such as myself. Inevitably Michael Palin had beaten me to it and he showed me his letter.

To put all of this in context. The Chinese accept a blend of western and traditional medicine; medical students study both and pharmacies are divided into two sections; the familiar shelves stacked with packets and boxes bearing the logos of giant drugs conglomerates and the other part which has large ceramic pots and wooden boxes filled with curious powders, roots, fungus, barks, dried leaves, caterpillars and ground scorpions. It seems that people use whatever remedy is most appropriate. Children with a sore throat drink water in which has been placed what looks like a tree gall. Teachers boil garlic in vinegar in classrooms to produce a foul-smelling general prophylactic against winter germs. Persistent conditions are treated with antibiotics delivered via canula and drip. There is not the narrow mistrust of alternative therapies that is practiced in Europe and the USA by mainstream medicos.

What makes Dr. Ho remarkable here in China is his extensive and specialized knowledge and the range of medical conditions he claims to have cured. Quack or legitimate healer? As he wrapped a wad of healthy tea for me this is immaterial. If it works for the people who had come to him from thousands of miles away, then let his expertise be fostered and continue.

Charlotte's Chinese New Year – an interlude

Charlotte is a colleague who was invited by someone she met on a train to celebrate the big family celebration of New Year in Jiangsu province, near a town called Xuzhou. The experience was unforgettable and she tells it in her own words:

"My friend lives in a village and I had no idea what to expect. She and her family live in a courtyard style home which was nice but freezing. Everyday I was wearing 7 layers of clothes on my top half, 3 layers on my bottom half and about 4 pairs of socks. It was absolutely normal to sit in the house with coats and hats on; we went to a few relatives' and neighbours' houses and they were all doing the same. The have the front doors open and shiver away and they are still happy and laughing and not complaining like we do in Britain. I have never been so cold for so long in my life, the warmest place was in bed!

They also didn't have a bathroom, so when I first got there and needed the toilet, my friend had to get a torch and take me to the public toilet which had no lighting in it; I had never been to a toilet like that before. There were concrete blocks to stand on, then you would squat and go to the toilet; there were no doors or partitions, presumably to make it easier to have a conversation with the person next to you. A couple of days later I found out that they have an outside toilet at their home. It is behind a storage building and had no roof and just a couple of stones to stand on. It is very difficult to try and undo your trousers and squat when it is cold and snowing and you can hardly move because of the seven layers you are wearing.

They also had no bath so we had to go to the public baths for a shower and that happened once a week, so in my fortnight stay I only showered twice, and mostly wore the same clothes; it was rather nice not caring about how you looked or smelt. The public showers were a bit of an experience, the first time wasn't so bad because not many people were there and we spent an hour in the shower washing and eating oranges, and I didn't want to leave because it was so nice and hot. The second time was a lot more scary. I went with my friend's mother to the shower and this time it was really busy and the other women were staring at me as I was undressing and in the shower; as you can imagine it was very unnerving. All the showers were taken, but one women let me share with her. Then the mother came to scrub my back; she scrubbed my back, my bottom and my legs, and every inch of fat on my body was wobbling from it, and the Chinese women, were all watching. I was quite traumatised by that experience.

The family was very kind to me, and kept feeding me, and did not allow me to help or do anything. I felt like a goose that was being force-fed ready to be made into fois gras; it was quite nice but undid all my work of going to the gym. I am amazed that the Chinese, as a race, are so thin because they are constantly eating. At meal times they eat a lot and in-between meals they are constantly eating, fruit, nuts, seeds, sweets, anything! Even in the shower they eat, It's amazing; my friend is so small and yet eats so much! I think I met the whole family; we went visiting to see aunts and uncles and cousins and grandparents. They are all the same, very kind and force feeding you; every time we left the house to go somewhere, my pockets would be stuffed with food, apples, oranges, nuts raisins, we would go to a house and have more food given. One day we visited her mother's side of the family in another village. The grandparents lived in a little old cottage, quite run down and the grandmother kept laughing at me and speaking to me but we couldn't understand each other at all. They

57

were very kind. The village was poorer than the one my friend lived in wit lots of animals about and dirt tracks instead of concrete.

I am really loving Chinese food, especially the delicious dumplings which I had for breakfast most mornings. I learnt quite a lot about Chinese life and culture. People are quite amazing in that they get on with life and don't complain and find a lot of simple things to entertain themselves with. They are so friendly and kind. The family took very good care of me and were very protective of me. They considered me to be part of the family – like another daughter - which was nice. I was included in the annual family photograph; it's odd to look at with me on the end, taller than by twice the size of everyone else. The family couldn't speak English, so communicating with them, especially with my bad Chinese was quite difficult. I knew "hello" "thank you" a rude way of saying "going to the toilet" "idiot" and "brainless." Not really conversational Chinese but it made them laugh. The father knew "ok" and "please sit down" the mother nothing and the brother "go", "WC" and "oh my god." I had a cough when I was there and they gave me some medicine and the next day I was better. I am now nice and relaxed and in good health and back from my travels. Soon work will start, which will be strange because I haven't been working for over a month."

LIJIANG, DALI & YANGSHUO

Lijiang (Lee-jang), *Dali* (Dar-lee), and *Yangshuo* (Yung-show), in Western china are all on the backpacker's trail.

Pretty *Lijiang* in Northern Yunan has an extensive old city saved from a recent earthquake and mercifully free of high rise buildings or grid pattern. Instead the dwellings bear the stamp of the *Naxi* ethnic minority; two storey wooden constructions with balconies and arranged around a courtyard. These creaking structures make for splendid accommodation so different from the customary diet of bland shiny hotels. The chaotic street layout, which is impossible to navigate, is dictated by the delta of fast-flowing channels of clear water which course down from the mountains around. Nearly every shop here plays to the tourist decorated with lanterns and selling silks, pottery, carvings, clothes. It is most pleasant to sit at a streamside café or balcony restaurant in the winter sunshine and watch the world pass by. Beyond the city is the white cap of Jade Dragon Snow Mountain.

Moving upstream towards the mountain one comes to a park on the northern limits of the city. It is a classic; crystal clear lake, elegant bridges, pavilions with upturned roofs and planted with willows. The *Naxi* or *Dongba* culture is represented in a corner of this park. I have seen their buildings and costume and heard their language and music – there is a nightly concert in the town. Here there is a *Dongba* wiseman who is one of the few members of this ethnic minority that can use their writing system. Highly stylized Chinese characters were developed and refined from pictographs over the centuries so that you can now barely see their pictorial origins. *Dongba* pictographs are mostly all transparently obvious. A deer looks like – well, a deer. House, man, lake look like just those things. This of course gives the writing form a universality as anyone can understand the symbols whatever their native tongue. On the other hand, as far as I could ascertain, lacking a grammar or much beyond what we would recognise as nouns it lacks the fundamentals to express anything beyond the simple or transactional present.

The trip south to Dali takes one through a broad valley with the most magnificent scenery – mountains, lakes, terraced slopes and villages of courtyard houses. Dali itself has a rougher beauty; it has its tourist spots but seems to be more of a working town. Contained within a wall between a lake on the east and a mountain range to the west it is less sanitised than *Lijiang* with dwellings that look less well kempt and in some ways more interesting. Buses ply up and down the dust road outside the city wall and mounds of stone litter the place ready to be turned into the marble baubles for which *Dali* is famous. Apart from three-dimensional shapes large and small, craftsmen produce screens of marble engrained with black red and grey wavy patterns – marbling in fact! There is a tourist area and there is also an area that caters for western backpackers – good-quality but cheap hotels and restaurants with English menus. In fact the ethnic iconography of these places, western rock issuing from doorways and signs such as "drumming this afternoon" suggested how I imagine Haight Ashbury was in the 70's. Although a walk along the well-paved western range of mountains is not a wilderness experience it is nonetheless a dramatic 10km. At about 1000m above the town this path, often with railings, weaves in and out of deep ravines with sheer drops below and snowmelt waterfalls tumbling off the peaks above.

If *Lijiang* and *Dali* are touristy, *Yangshuo* is full-on in your face western. The co-incidentally named "West Street" unashamedly offers bars, cafes and hotels catering for gap year students. Language schools abound trading on the necessity of local shop assistants to speak English. I suppose the Cost del Sol is a bit like this! Although amongst all of the croissants and muesli breakfasts it is not exclusively European I wonder if half the attraction for the Chinese that make it here is to mingle with foreigners in this theme park version of western life. This is probably the nearest that most of them will ever get to Europe or the States; a passport costs a relatively steep 200yuan (£15) but the remaining finances are even more formidable. The present exchange rate means that £4.00 can buy you a basic room and bathroom for the night - £1.00 if you want a bed in a shared room. Compare that with the cheapest bed in an English youth hostel which is about £16.00. In China 2000 yuan or £130.00 per month is considered to be a good salary.

The beauty of *Yangshuo* lies in its extraordinary landscape. Firstly it is on the bend of the wide and fast-flowing river *Li*. Secondly a sub-tropical climate engenders palm trees and other exotica. But the most astonishing feature here is the limestone karst scenery. Huge mounds of rock from the size of a large house to several hundred metres high dot the otherwise flat plain. Roads, rivers and buildings weave their way between these formations which are variously like cones, columns, stacks, some regular shapes others distorted. All of them luxuriantly draped with plants and foliage. On the flat ground buffalo browse or pull ploughs through the hard-working soil in readiness for rice or other crops while the karsts punctuate the land in a willfully profligate manner serving no purpose other than to attract tourists. Some earn their keep by providing a novelty scenic spot in a park with steps cut into them and pavilions set on ledges; others by their curious shape such as half-moon hill to which I cycled to see the beautifully regular archway right through the rock. From the summit of this one the karsts stretched away into the mist and the distance on the flat land like turned earth on a lawn with a particularly virulent attack of moles.

A popular evening trip is to take a boat to watch cormorant fishing. As in other parts of the world these birds are trained to catch fish but are prevented from eating them by having a cord tied round their gullet. Unlike the cormorants I swallowed my ethics and took my place on the passenger boat. Another boat with two high wattage lamps raced downstream, us following. The owner set the birds on the prow and we watched as they dived in swimming at least as fast as the boat to resurface fifteen seconds later returning to their owner who would massage the fish out of the birds' throats. We were told that the birds are allowed to eat every seventh fish. As a piece of history or man in communion with nature: impressive. The birds appeared sleek and in good health. I had rather dismissed this as simply something put on for the tourists, but the next morning as I ate my breakfast in a café overlooking the river there below me was a couple of fishermen on bamboo rafts poling their way upstream and each with a couple of birds at attention on the front.

I dearly wanted to spend more time here but against all reason – it is over an hour's flight south of *Dali* – it was bitterly cold. I now regretted the haircut that I had had in Hong Kong and bought a woollen hat. I could fly to the sunny southern beaches of *Hainan* or visit the jungle on the Vietnam border – but I had to go somewhere warm

"*Fahlon, fahlon, fahlon*" I am sure that this is what she said because she repeated it so many times. According to my instructions I should get off the train at *Ningming,* find the river and embark on a boat but this woman was taking me away from the river. If it had been in the United States *Ningming* would be called a one-horse town; it had two streets, a factory and a pig rooting around outside the station. The only help I had received so far was from a beaming railway official who had almost sent me back one station up the line, and a slightly more helpful lady who had cancelled this just as the train drew in and pointed me in the direction of the river. I ignored the *fahlon* lady for a bit as I couldn't fit either her or "*fahlon*" into my scheme of things. She was still there though when I approached a boatmen and she and he seemed to agree that whatever she proposed was the thing that I wanted. Gesturing back towards the road – *fahlon, fa*hlon – and taking a sceptical me with her, I could only think that somehow she knew my destination and perhaps knew enough English to tell me that it was a long way from here.

She stopped a passing motor-rickshaw and had an animated discussion with the driver and with much nodding they also seemed to agree that whatever she proposed was the thing that I wanted. She and I, maintaining my scepticism, climbed into the rickshaw and back we went, past the station, past the pig, over the railway lines and factory and out of the town onto a newish road. I love this low jungle scenery, palms, bamboo, and red earth bare where it is not being cultivated. It had been fascinating like this all the way from *Nanning*, passing small towns and settlements, paddies and ponds and as we neared *Ningming* the re-emergence of the karst formations that had been so much a part of the landscape of *Yangshuo*. Here it was mostly flat as we found our way back onto the flood-plain of the river with sharply rearing mountains at the edges.

After a twenty minute journey the road finished, the lady took me through a gateway and thankfully I found myself at my intended destination.

It is possible to arrive at *Panlong* by boat, but evidently the preferred route is the new road. The only thing at the small village of *Panlong* is the hotel and by Chinese standards this is quite special: 3 traditional *Zhuang* houses removed and rebuilt here provide the accommodation. Wonderfully solid yet creaky wooden structures, they are full of character and have large rooms with balconies. A flashy new concrete hotel sits opposite underneath a hill, but is not yet in use. The guide who took me in hand explained that "*fahlon*" was just the way some local people pronounced "*Panlong*." In China I had been getting used to variable vowels, but I felt that shifting consonants was a bit much!

The hotel generally received guests who were part of a guided tour and at this moment it was, apart from my presence, completely empty. My own attempts to join such a tour in *Nanning* had met with blank looks from the cluster of travel agents that I had visited. Some professed never to have heard of this site. After I had signed in and had lunch a man appeared who, it transpired, was Mr. *Fahlon*. He offered to take me upstream in his boat. Things now started to fall into place. I could see that his wife's guiding me to this place might not have been completely altruistic! Although I thought his price of 100yuan a bit steep the guide assured me this was OK.

We walked to the river past a rusting novelty boat embellished with dragon head and tail. His more modest vessel was like a large version of a punt with a shelter in the middle. We puttered out into the middle of the stream and drove up the middle of the river with about 50 metres of water on either side. On the banks clumps of great bamboo-like plants prospered with occasional stems lying dead flat on the ground. Beyond them were the fields and beyond them the sharp mountains. Every so often a boat would pass either with tourists or with nets strung out front for fish but mostly we had the river to ourselves. Perhaps I had seen the Vietnam War film "Apocalypse Now" too many times, but that was the scenery that I was reminded of and with the Vietnamese border less than 30 miles to the west it wasn't surprising. After about forty minutes the river veered around great limestone cliffs and I expected to see the way barred with Kurt's henchmen. Instead, on the right bank a great white wall of stone – *Hua Shan* - reared up and on it were hundreds of petroglyphs. They were all in red with the recurring motif of a human with arms raised at right angles from the elbows and mirrored symmetrically by the legs. Their provenance is uncertain although they are considered to be connected with the local Zhuang culture but part of the mystery is simply how and why they came to be painted in such an inaccessible location; they range from about twenty metres up to maybe sixty. The boatman cut the engine and we swung and drifted in the current underneath the cliff.

On the return to *Panlong* we picked up four men. For one of them the concept of a human who was unable to speak or understand Mandarin was beyond his experience and he gamely kept addressing me, each time a little louder; a sort of Chinese version of Colonel Blimp. Nevertheless when they saw me parting with a 100yuan note at the end of the trip they made it quite clear that 50yuan would have sufficed. Just a few nights previously a similar trip had cost me 30yuan, but as there were at least twenty others on that boat I had reckoned that 100yuan was good value for this trip where I had the boat mostly to myself! As someone adrift in an alien economy this will always be a problem; I was not generally taken for a ride though and more often was the recipient of generosity and good will.

It was such a peaceful spot that I was very happy to spend the next day there. Behind the hotel buildings was the mountain wall which marked the limit of the flood plain. A stair had been hacked up this wall at one point and after a stiff climb to a pass one left one world and entered another. Behind were cultivated fields, river traffic, motor rickshaws and the detritus of civilization. Ahead though was the sort of wild terrain that only ever exists in adventures: closely packed ridges and domes of rock too steep to ascend and covered on every surface with trees and shrubs. This was Boys Own territory, jungle for 18th century explorers. The *Longrui* Reserve is home to the white-headed leaf monkey, an island in the otherwise densely packed province for these creatures to escape extinction. With some trepidation I entered the area as there was no way that one could take bearings; forest was around me for most of the time and when up high or in a clearing the cliffs gave no landmark, but only a sense of the vastness of the area as the peaks misted into infinity. It was too good to miss however and I plunged along the tracks enjoying the smell of rotting plant and damp wood. I enjoyed the exuberance of the vegetation growing on every available surface in a myriad of manifestations. I enjoyed the isolation. A thoroughly enjoyable day and the tracks got me back too of course. Sadly I didn't spot any of the monkeys, or indeed any wildlife apart from birds. That came later.

Taking a shower that evening, I noticed that the spray was spilling onto the bedroom carpet. I had not noticed this the previous day and had left the door open. Being a good guest I swung the door to. To my consternation something lurked – that is the operative word – lurked on the door, close to the hinge at eye level. Moving closer revealed in the steamy atmosphere the black body, four legs stretched out front and four legs stretched out back; the size of my hand. Something about its uniformity and the almost comic mode of my discovering it made me rationalize it into a joke spider; a rubber effigy stuck to the door by a fun-loving employee. No real spider would be that symmetrical and be discovered in such a trite way. Looking back on it now I realize I was in denial! I finished my shower in a very British way and gingerly opened the door (just in case) dried myself and put on my glasses. Re-entering the shower-room was worse as spider (if it was real) might have moved and have the advantage over me. As I edged round the door spider was still there (can't be real). Maintaining my Britishness I studied the object carefully. It was superbly moulded and imperceptibly fixed to the door. Closer inspection revealed the fine hairs on the legs – overdoing the detail a bit I thought. What finally convinced me though was the thread issuing from the abdomen. I looked anxiously for any signs of biting or injecting equipment it might possess, but not sure what form this might take I remained ignorant of its degree of lethalness. Spider, meanwhile, remained quite motionless (could it be fake?). I could leave spider alone as it didn't seem highly active and had presumably been there the previous night while I slept blissfully unaware. That of course was the difference – now I was aware and would never sleep. Even if spider did not walk over my defenceless face in the middle of the night it might change location so that I would never be at peace again in the room.

One of the most disquieting things about many insects and spiders is their unpredictability. Bears and lions hurtle and lunge straight at you. There is no dispute about your fate and you just have to be resigned. Spiders react irrationally. When I attempted to brush it into an empty drawer spider reacted instantly and so fast that I don't remember seeing the movement. A slight change of position on the door and its legs moved from out front and back to straight out either side. I remember wondering if spider could hear my heart beating and my shallow breathing. I eventually coaxed spider into the drawer where it remained for the night, safely covered. The next morning after breakfast and with a slight feeling of mastery I removed spider in a plastic bag to some shrubs about 100 metres behind the hotel and released it, wondering if it would make its way back there. I did wonder though, if I should have reapplied spider to the door as a sort of joke for the next inhabitant of my room. Imagine their surprise when they swung the door . . .

ENGLISH CORNER

Back in Weifang the weather which had had a promise of spring all week was colder, much colder. Standing in the park for two hours would necessitate the donning of my thermal underwear I decided. Laundry today. The good news is that the one washing machine for everyone is located in the dormitory next door to me, the bad news - the door is locked and I have to go in search in the biting February wind for the janitor. After a full day yesterday, which itself followed a very late night I am still tired as I breakfast western style on muesli and bread and marmalade; the limited facilities in the apartment deny me the luxury of toast. I arrange the washed clothes on the heating pipes in the apartment to dry and at 9.30 I leave.

The fleet of No.16 buses has recently been upgraded and a smart green one draws up at the stop the same time as I do. This driver though is in a hurry and the twenty minute journey takes ten with more than the usual amount of horn blowing and lurching. His haste is infectious and passengers move rapidly on and off. I leap into the street that, unusually for grid-patterned Weifang, forms a serpentine route between two principal roads and is enhanced with a lively market. Although it is February the fruit in season is strawberry, forced I am told in the poly-tunnels one sees at the side of the expressway. The fruits are large and generally taste watery so I see no reason to doubt this. I dive down a short cut past some caged chickens and bonsai trees and up the road to Dong Yuan Park.

"English Corner" is a quaintly Chinese institution, I think. In towns all over China at a designated spot and time people who wish to practice their English will gather whatever the weather and speak to each other. The larger cities which boast English-speaking foreigners draw them into this process as role models. It is an expression of the community ethic, of how skills are shared, in the same way that in the country harvest is still a communal activity. It is also an expression of how desperate people are to learn the language; English is the key to better jobs, better pay, travel possibilities and status. There are many small language schools which trade on this need and I have known friends to be approached by complete strangers in restaurants and asked if they would tutor a son or daughter. Chinese schools teach the written language with more or less efficiency but what people lack is real-life speakers of the language. The utter disbelief that people exhibit at the sight of a Westerner walking Weifang's streets underlines this.

As I approach the designated spot in the park the twenty or so individuals of all ages who are talking to each other in groups break up and coalesce into one large circle around me and we greet each other. At this point I always feel uncomfortable because what had been half a dozen lively conversations is now one conversation observed by twenty people. True, it is nice to be the centre of attention but the teacher in me tells me that this is not the most active way to learn whatever the compensation of hearing my home-counties accent. Nevertheless I plunge on and the theme this week turns to food, the question of kitchen hygiene in Chinese and English restaurants, the greater variety and skills of Chinese chefs; I realise that the group equates Western food with pizza, Macdonalds and KFC and soundly disabuse them of such an outrageous idea. Despite the popularity of such food in China I also demonstrate firm support of their own food culture which is vastly superior.

The most common question asked is "What do you think of Weifang?" I can only answer this in terms of my own expectations and tell them truthfully that it is a very pleasant city and very friendly. I qualify this by telling them that I prefer the countryside and explain how it is possible to live a sophisticated life in the English countryside as well as enjoying rural pleasures. This would be quite impossible in China. There is the countryside which equates to hard manual labour in fields and basic habitations, and there are the cities with restaurants, bright lights and the possibility of social progression. I also tell them of my preference for a more interesting landscape – Weifang is very flat. This leads onto a discussion of other interesting places in their country. Some of them, surprisingly, have travelled extensively around the country, but most of them have not ventured outside Shandong, *Qingdao* on the coast being a popular destination. Nevertheless most of them know about the interesting spots such as the holy mountains, HangShan, WutaiShan, and scenic areas such as JiuzhaiGou and Zhangjiajie. For some of them making the cultural shift from the countryside to the city has been a substantial one. We touch on politics – they agree there is too much corruption, the media often carry stories about this – but they are not overly worried about having no voting power. The ensuing Olympics are a matter of great pride; as nations we are joined in this as the subsequent games will be held in the UK. They want to know what I think of their games logo. Privately I think that the five cartoon characters seen constantly on TV now are sentimental and insipid versions of the Rice Crispies frontmen: *Snap, Crackle* and *Pop*. Chinese advertising is like this though – softer, more pastel and innocent with much less hard sell or cleverness. I tell the crowd that I think the logo is inspired. The talk continues and their understanding of many issues is at least as advanced as thinking in the west. They are acutely aware of the environmental problems facing them, of pollution and of water shortage. They are shocked and disbelieving when I tell them about urban decay in the UK and the appalling level of youth crime, despair and unemployment. Their own town has many grubby areas but here it is for want of money not because of vandalism. Although there is poverty here, people seem to maintain a doggedness in the face of adversity sustained by strong family ties, but mostly there is optimism. When I talk about conditions in English schools and the poor attitudes from students it is beyond their comprehension. All of them have an enormous faith in the power of education and if they are not in full-time education themselves it is likely that they are studying for some further qualification. They are keen to hear about my family and about how people live. There is an intense curiosity about life beyond China that cannot be satisfied through books or the media. After a couple of hours of this grilling I am beginning to be quite light-headed.

As if on cue a colleague appears and tells me that I have been invited to lunch by the parent of one of my pupils. Now. This is the way that a lot of things happen here but this invitation cuts across a previous arrangement I have made. With slight misgiving I cut short my time in the park – I have been there for over an hour - and agree to return to my host after a book purchase. When I locate the restaurant, the usual gilt and chrome encrusted hangar, I find father and 12 year old daughter are already entertaining both my colleague and another lively and articulate friend from English Corner. My host is in a senior position in a clothing factory which includes customers such as the UK cosmetic firm Avon on its books. He has traveled in the course of his business more widely than I have and is enthused with the entrepreneurial spirit that is now the epitome of China. He assures me that the 800 workers in his factory are rewarded for innovative ideas but is also personally aware of the toll that business pressures place on him.

He is at the beck and call of Western companies who expect him to be available in their time zone.

On another occasion another acquaintance tells me tales, as we sit next to the old gate into the city, of how the communists dug a tunnel under the river and wall in order to liberate it from the *Goumindong*. He tells me about his grandfather, a landlord who had his house and lands confiscated by the communists and was reduced to a street cleaner. Other members of the family lost their factory but were given two rooms in the building in which to live. News of another relation came recently whose grave was discovered in the south. He had been fighting against the *Goumingdong* when they fled to Taiwan. People in his family had to destroy photographs of relations or other evidence that would tie them to the ruling class. All this was a time of great leveling. Three generations later he himself is a successful entrepreneur and I have seen Maseratis in the showrooms with a price tag of three million yuan. If his grandfather were still cleaning the streets he would take home about 400 yuan a month.

Sunday; passing afternoons after lunch in the spotless people's park full to the brim with bridal parties and photographers or trawling the markets to view curiosities; learning about the fortune-tellers or chess players on the pavements. More wealth for more people but still the simple pleasures.

Despite the fact that *Weifang,* a city of six million souls, does not feature on any tourist itinerary and is relatively unknown, it is a thriving metropolis in the fertile province of *Shandong*, Eastern China. Its claim to fame is that it is the Kite Capital of the World. The kite symbol adorns public buses and buildings, kites are on sale everywhere and are often to be seen in the sky being flown from the many parks. A strong prevailing wind from the west, sometimes gritty, at times warm buoys them up.

Although I have a natural resistance to something as apparently pointless as kites, I begin my education with a visit to the museum. The building first of all impresses with large wall murals, traditional curve-up roof and magnificent water frontage. Galleries surround an atrium courtyard with a suspended kite. In the west displays would have been more interactive but there is a primitive charm in the presentation of shapes, patterns, styles and materials. Very finely painted images with cultural references on material such as paper or silk stretched over a framework of bamboo strips dominate. The designs often dictate the aerodynamics. Some ingenious kites have moving effects and some use the wind to drive wheels, for instance on painted carriages, or to harness the power from the windmill, to move legs, eyes and beaks via a crank: and remember all this has to be light enough to stay in the air. A workshop reveals a master kite-maker at his craft.

This is not a minority interest but a thriving industry in which modern designs manufactured here sell for a good price abroad. During a trip to the desert in the saltpan north of *Shandong* Pansheng, who owns such a company, allows me to put his models through their paces. Frameless and made of strong ripcord, they are similar in shape to a modern parachute canopy, rigidity coming from wind-filled tubes in the fabric. Four cords control movement laterally and vertically. Certainly on this outing it is a joyous experience to battle with the wind and move the kites at will around the sky. Such is their design logic that when they become grounded a twitch on the right cords gets them airborne again without the bore of finding someone to yield it to the sky. "Battle" is not an inappropriate word as the kites often drag one along the ground in the seemingly moderate wind and more than once I drop to the sand on my back in order to anchor the kite. On another trip to *Yantai* on the coast I see similar models used to power a three-wheel truck across the beach. Pansheng sells on the internet abroad only and has made a good business out of it. He jealously guards his designs from others.

As the April Kite Festival approaches the whole city goes into hyperdrive. Workers everywhere are to be seen washing the facades of public buildings and hotels, flowers and trees are planted along the approach roads, new parks are completed including the kite park next to the museum complete with life-size bronze mannequins making kites and music activated fountains. Thousands of people are expected to fill the hotels; several hundred foreigners will come too and students from the university are co-opted to guide them and interpret for them. Concerts and civic functions are organized to complement the festival.

Ten kilometers from the city at *Fuyan Shan*, a mild blip in the *Shandong* plain, a new observation tower has been built to view the kites. This is where the festival proper takes place. Arriving there on the day of the festival along with the rest of the city, the mood is contagious and high – like the kites. On a vast field in front of the tower everyone is milling and in the sky the kites are milling too. The most impressive include a 600 metre dragon kite and 3D animals. The former has a head facing the flier and then a string of small circular vanes connected together in a line behind it forming the tail. This is a prototype; the next one will be two thousand metres. The animals featured have a cunning system of vents and valves which enables the wind to both inflate and also keep them airborne. Lesser kites are vast box-structures with pictures of gods on them or utilize the wind to produce a sound like that of a small aircraft as they dive about the field. To complete the sense of carnival in the sky on the ground there are displays of drumming and dancing in an area demarcated by lines of soldiers on low stools who squat to attention unsmiling.

For the rest of the spring and summer the lazy weekend afternoon skies are dotted with kites flown by men or boys from the parks and squares in the city. A mild and innocent pleasure. China's relaxations are of a different magnitude to those of the west where leisure is frenetically mediated by higher forms of technology. Kites might attract a sneering attitude from those who believe they are further up civilization's ladder. Actually though not so different from fishing, I would imagine, in its ability to free the mind from trivia and provide a chance to contemplate the depths or soar the heights. They are relatively inexpensive, cost nothing to run, do not pollute, do not harm animals and are attractive. Bring on the kites!

Walking the streets you pass them. They sit silently on pavements outside shops or in corners on bridges. Sometimes they kowtow their heads low on the pavement never lifting their eyes in a gesture of abject submission that owes more to a feudal nineteenth century than the progressive policies of the twenty-first.

Sometimes they let tarred and truncated limbs speak for them, sometimes they sit with a written journal of their misfortune in front of them and sometimes their children pester you. In Shanghai tiny children perform acrobatics. Grasping a swivel on a discarded chair base they flip their bodies over their heads and spin grotesquely. The damage to teeth and neck muscles must be incalculable. They come at you holding grubby plastic mugs for a few jiao. Beggars, in China as in the west.

Lu Xun is not his name as I forgot to ask it but it is better than an impersonal label. He sits on the road leading from the kite museum, thin blue trousers and jacket and peaked Mao-style cap, one crutch by his side. *Lu* is an affable speaker, loquacious and open, his face weathered and his teeth witness to poor nutrition and health care. He is not a native of *Weifang* but has come all of the way from *Gansu*, a province far in the North on the edge of Mongolia. He lives in an inhospitable mountain region which is cold for much of the year and can only manage one harvest of a crop known as *dongui*. Life is very tough. He leaves his wife at the thinnest of times to eke a living by begging in the more prosperous southern provinces and possibly to avoid the shame of begging in a town where he might be recognized. If he is lucky he might collect 8 or 10 yuan in a day which is enough for him to buy some food, otherwise he will go hungry. Ten yuan is equivalent to 70 pence. I learn this on the same day that I read that the average Briton spent £7,000 last year on consumer goods. At night he sleeps in the bus station. *Lu Xun* is 68 years old which puts his birth in the troubled times of the Japanese occupation with an alliance of the nationalist GMD forces and Mao's communists in control of the mid-western city of *Chongqing*. He suffered an injury to his leg whilst serving as a soldier, presumably during the North Korean war of the 50s.

New apartments on the other side of the river from where we are talking are advertised at a rent of 3,000 yuan a month, there are more cars on the roads each year, China's trade surplus is immense and growing. Common people earn very little – mostly less than 1,000 a month – and manage on it. There is no social security payment and health care has to be paid for. It seems difficult to reconcile the two facts of increasng wealth on the one hand and poverty beyond the experience of most westerners on the other. *Lu Xun*, appears to be unaware of the incongruency of the two extremes. He has lived through the turbulence of foreign invasions, civil war and the roller-coaster epoch of *Mao Zedong*. He has nothing but fulsome praise for the present regime and is optimistic that China is now on the right path.

With so many climatic regions and so many ethnic minorities the range of food is enormous, but I haven't yet encountered dishes which equate to those on offer from Chinese restaurants in the UK; not even in *Guangzhou* from where the English/Chinese style of cooking – Canton – is presumed to come.

Culinary machinery is adapted to produce the regional delicacies. In *Suzhou* an iron plate with many deep conical pods is heated; into each pod is put a mixture of batter, chopped figs and other fruits; when cooked the now solid cone is eased out and offered for sale in a twist of grey paper. A similar process but with hemispherical pods exists in Shanghai, and there they are filled with scraps of meat and turned to produce a more consistently cooked offering. In *Shandong* pancakes are popular; nearly two feet across they are cooked on large hotplates and filled thickly with chopped spring onion. However in *Tai'an* pancakes are thinner and crepe-like, with cooks using a wooden leveler like the French, but in this case the hotplate is spun like a potter's wheel, while the stationary leveler skims off the excess batter.

In *Guangxi* a stove has a number of burners and a corresponding number of holes in the metal cover. The holes receive a clay pot which contains an individual casserole. The lidded pot is delivered to your table. An extension of this idea is the self-choice hotpot; diners sit at tables with integral burners which keep a soup piping hot; you choose a savoury or spicy soup. You also choose a range of vegetables and meats that you then cook in the bubbling broth in front of you.

Breads may be baked in conventional ovens but many are steamed in great tiers of steamers: steamed buns of different shapes and complexions and also dumplings filled with meat or a mixture of egg and vegetable.

In addition to this variety there is the ubiquitous use of the wok on a range with a naked coal flame which is blown to a wicked heat with an electric fan; food is cooked quickly and is often in front of you within five minutes of ordering. To achieve this level of efficiency food is chopped into sizes according to their cookability; tomatoes, which cook easily, are in large chunks but potatoes, which are more dense, are chopped into impossibly thin slices so that everything ends up taking about the same time to cook. Favourite accompaniments to flavour dishes are peanut butter, garlic, aniseed, soy and peppers.

Many restaurants have pictures of their dishes or even raw ingredients ready on plates under cling-film which is an aid for a non-Chinese speaker when ordering. Vegetables and fruit are greater in range than in the UK: plants collected from local mountains, mulberry leaves, and lotus roots for instance. Likewise for meat-eaters the range knows no limits from flying squirrels to salamanders. I have seen alligators being hacked up and snakes waiting their turn. Worms and grubs, crunchy cicadas and scorpions. Dog. On one occasion a dish was placed next to me with a flourish and there, its head and legs hanging limply over the edges of the rim was a tortoise. Fish are displayed in great banks of aquaria languidly waiting to be eaten; most are conventional with mouths and fins but there are often nightmarish things too with spines and tendrils which suck their way along the inside of the glass.

For a banquet you need a private room in a restaurant, a round table and congenial company. Dishes that have been ordered - soups, vegetables, fish, groundnuts, fruits - arrive as they are cooked and are placed on the lazy susan. Diners spin this and pick up whatever they wish directly with their chopsticks from the serving dishes. I have passed my Key Stage 3 in chopsticks. It's like riding a bike –once you stop to think about how it works, it stops working. Soups are served into small individual bowls. Tea is usually served along with wine, beer or the local spirit. Rice is rarely served unless requested. If hunger has not been satisfied final dishes of noodles or dumplings might be called for. The idea of separate courses does not exist and when the meal, sans pudding, sans cheese is finished there is no relaxed talk over coffee and liqueurs because they don't exist either. People simply leave.

Teaching in Weifang was for me a high energy activity. I have never been a sedentary teacher but the demands of the situation here seemed to require maximum effort. The thirteen year olds were mostly a pleasant bunch but for some of them it was difficult to sustain attention for forty minutes when their command of English was poor. In the UK I used the board very little, but here it was essential and I must have got through a whole quarry of chalk - blackboards are still in use. I learnt to write clearly and to draw, after a fashion and also to play the penny whistle.

Before each lesson I would write the topics vocabulary on the board and then draw animals, pictures of weather types or whatever was needed. The lesson would begin with a whole class introduction or revision of the vocabulary, and then I would point at random individuals to ensure that they had mastered the words. Then I would practice phrases and move on to a set question and answer session. "What is the weather like today?" I would beam whilst violently gesturing to the wind outside the window. "What is my job?" I would ask while miming a crazy pilot wrestling with a control column. "What do you find on a farm?" I would say while moo-ing like a cow. I'm sure the entertainment value of all this was tremendous as I rarely had anyone fall asleep in class. Sometimes I reversed the role and got pupils to pick a job or animal and mime it for the class instead.

I found myself using teaching methods from a century ago to get the point over. Chanting and repetition were on their way out when I started school, but here, with such large classes and few other options it was essential.

> Good morning. Good morning
> How-do-you-do?

Good morning, I'm fine
How about you?

Or

The animals went in two by two
Hurrah hurrah
The animals went in two by two
Hurrah hurrah
The animals went in two by two
The elephant and the kangaroo
And they all went marching down

For which I learnt the tune and accompanied them on the penny whistle. With large classes it was essential that I maintain such an active role to make sure that they paid attention to me. As soon as I asked a question the pupil would stand and give an answer. There was never any derision from fellow pupils if the answer was wrong and so in the main pupils never felt self-conscious about answering. They had a course book to follow, which was just about right for them in terms of difficulty and age, and they had me careering round the room like a character from a pantomime.

It was important for me to invent commands or gestures early on that they could learn and respond to as well as lesson patterns that they became accustomed to so that all went smoothly. I tried to ensure that I was never in a situation where they would not understand what I required from them. When that happened the whole momentum of the lesson collapsed. A whole mad compendium of body-language was developed which indicated "stand-up," "sit-down," "you repeat," "all repeat" and so on. They seemed to be able to identify numbers or count in sequence, but when I required them to look at their books I had to hold up the page and parade frenetically around the room to ensure that they found the right one. Another problem arose from poor eyesight. Many of them simply could not see any detail on the board and quite often had to come to the front to answer a question about a word or a drawing.

Most of the teaching you will gather, was to understand vocabulary in context, simple phrases in common usage and to be able to ask and answer questions. There were also simple stories with a highly controlled vocabulary from which understanding could be wrought. The stories were at a very lowly level and usually involved talking animals or wizards. For the average ten-year old in Britain the content of these stories would have been fine, but in China where children remained younger for longer they were just about right for these thirteen-year olds. It was very pleasing to see that from these stories some pupils, at least, understood concepts of structure or character. Teaching is never value free and along with the words and stories the children were learning about England too. Will they grow up thinking that "How do you do" is a common greeting? If they visit will they expect wizards and hysterical princesses? Will they expect all English men to be hyperactive?

The end of term exam tested the vocabulary and for each of my three hundred and twenty pupils I had to award a mark out of one hundred. Because the school was regarded as a good school and parents paid 6,000 yuan per year – about £400.00 - to send their children there, all children were expected to gain at least 60%. No guidance on how to grade was available so it was up to my experience and professionalism. First I had to devise a class list from a written test. I ended up with three versions: Chinese characters, pinyin names – the anglicised form of the mandarin – and their English names. For each of my eight classes these last were almost identical. It seemed that someone had had a series of fifty names and doled them out to each class when the children entered the school. Some had names that had evolved from their Chinese names such as "Fly" or "Dragon." Some boys had girl's names and vice versa.

To make the test fair I devised a set routine of questions and most of the pupils seemed to have retained something. Some of the better pupils demonstrated their prowess by having extended conversations with me and using vocabulary beyond that used in the lessons. A very few of them stood before me and seemed to have learnt nothing at all. "What do you do before school?" I would quiz wildly mimimg teeth-brushing. "Lunch" they would reply. "What is the weather like?" I would ask gesturing expansively at the branches thrashing in the wind. "Yes I like weather" they would say. "What do you find in the country" I would try again. "No" would come the answer. There was nothing more I could do but award them a lowly 60 out of 100!

END OF TERM REPORT

The great thing you have to understand about the people of China is that they are so terribly secure. What is normally interpreted as inscrutability is the Chinese lack of demonstrability. Who needs to be demonstrative when you are sure about who you are and your place in the world? Shouting and waving your arms is for the insecure and those who show-off. Whatever happened to their society during the twentieth century it seemingly did not wipe out three thousand years of traditions, value systems or familial expectations. Maybe most significantly, older people are always revered and this is embedded in the language. Young people defer to them without question. Older people are perceived to be repositories of knowledge of preferred ways of living and their wisdom is valued. The young always defer to the old, the women to the men. When, god forbid, this natural order is upset there is only one outcome. It is deeply shaming for someone to lose face. Rare although it may be, if one person acts against the honour of another, then that person may restore the status quo – maybe with violence or a threat of it. If the matter is contestable then the violence can be extreme. I am thinking of the fight between two couples where the police arrived but did not intervene. The friends who witnessed this also witnessed the silent circle of onlookers watching, it seemed, some ancient justice or pecking order being established. They walked away when bricks started to be used.

Another illustration, this time in a bar where builders from the local site are taking a break at lunchtime. Four boys enter, clearly underage and not only breaking the law but also the social code. One of the workers asserts his right as an older person to instruct the younger and tells them they should not be there. They ignore him. Again, he tells them that the bar is for their fathers and uncles – not for them. Again no response. This puts the adult in a difficult situation as he is on the verge of losing face. He picks up a chair and with great fury smashes it on the counter, a piece of flying wood gashing him on the forehead. Brandishing the chair's remains he told them once more to leave. They leave like lambs and equilibrium is restored. Once in you must carry things through but in general everyone is careful not to let a situation get to the point of a showdown like this. Replay this scenario in an English pub and the outcome would be very different!

Why are the Chinese different? Their complete self-assurance and sense of security comes from two sources: their physical and social well being. In a quiet way the Chinese are fit and healthy. They move with care and with precision. I don't think I have yet seen anyone of any age fall or stumble. Young children sit astride luggage racks on bikes, adults sit sidesaddle with perfect balance. The fact that most sectors of the population cycle often contributes to health and well being. It is common to see children flexing their limbs by standing with one leg vertically above their heads. Adults stretch their legs against a tree. Everyone sits on small folding stools or squats. I have not seen anyone leaning or lounging – or strangely – running, other than in a race. I have been impressed by the speed at which children pick up Roman script – maybe because their hand-eye co-ordination has developed speedily through the far more complex learning of Chinese characters.

Children are exposed to the social milieu throughout their childhood. Children see whole universes of occupations around them all of the time as shopkeepers and artisans plying their trades are everywhere on the streets. Children notice implicitly or explicitly what is happening around them all of the time. It is quite in order for children – or adults – to stare at things which claim their attention. Moreover they SEE other people being sociable, and take this as a model for their own behavior later. Much of what happens in China happens outside, at least when the weather allows it, rather than behind doors in the sepulchral flicker of a cathode ray.

What is the nature of the street scene? Communal and spontaneous *tai ji*, dancing, music making to start with. Groups of men gathered around games of chess, cards or *mah jong*. Outdoor pool tables. Parks where people meet to talk or play co-operative games. Roller-blading squares. Often you will find men or women sitting solitarily, simply watching – there is no stigma in being alone – or in groups, maybe enjoying the songs of the captive birds they bring with them in cages.

Whilst the UK is awash with Asbos, gun crime and knifcrime, China is one of the safest countries I have ever visited. People are honest, they trust and are trusted. The drip-feed of moral values from older to younger ensures that social codes are transmitted with authority and universality. There are laws too of course, but it seems that every individual's self-discipline is much more important in keeping people on the straight and narrow as well as the regard of your peers. There is no mileage here in notoriety – you would become an outcast. When crimes are committed here, the police will sometimes have to investigate in order to discover the perpetrator, but more commonly, one person told me, the perpetrator, overcome with guilt, will give him or herself up. This is the power of unstated peer pressure. There still exists here a sense of society with strong and shared values.

The ramification of all this for young people is a period of growing up unhindered by many of the demons of the west. To start with the rite of passage that ends growing up, marriage, is placed somewhere after university and before the age of thirty. During this time young people are accountable to and financially dependent on their parents. A student confided that when his girlfriend visited they had shared a hotel room but did not have sex: the consequences for career, future prosperity and social disapproval of becoming pregnant would have been too appalling to contemplate. The older/younger rule means that all adults are obeyed – or at least far more so than in the UK. Children are told that the teacher is to be treated with the same respect as a parent. On the odd occasions when a child has to be reprimanded he or she responds with humility – not defiance – and other children keep a respectful distance to prevent the shame fall on them too. Secondly, the media has fewer representations of aggressive posturing or teenage sexuality which in turn means that there is virtually none of this in real life. Children enjoy – that word again – enjoy a childhood untainted with discussions of which is the coolest trainer; bullies are infrequent; minds are distracted by the opposite sex but probably less so and later. Instead their playtimes are joyful explosions of games of chance - paper, scissors, stone is popular - or physical dexterity – hoopla and yo-yo are the current rages. It is OK to be a child.

Perhaps the fact that their lives are highly orchestrated too is significant. Poorer children share the duties and responsibilities of agrarian families. Many children live in their schools for six days a week, rising at six and sleeping at eight. There is no opportunity to watch TV or hang around outside supermarkets. Moreover they are constantly in the company of their fellows, bred as social animals and constantly learning the checks and delays of communal living. They live in dormitories throughout their school years and live in dormitories at university and in the workplace too. They are taught in classes of 40+ rising to 150 at university. There may be a different attitude towards learning here but it certainly reinforces the group identity. People are keenly aware of others.

On the roads you can see the practical effects of this. Compared with the European individualistic mentality of "I'm following the rules so if you get in my way that will be your fault however badly you are hurt" the Chinese way is to be aware of who is in which part of the road and take necessary action. People are aware of obstructions and flaws in the pavement, of which there are many and take personal responsibility for avoiding them rather than taking the authorities to court for resulting accidents. Bicycles, pedestrians and cars weave in and out, with relative ease. I have often seen bicycles and cars moving contra-flow in a fast lane or appearing suddenly from a right-hand turn. Users placidly slow-down or make way for them. It looks like anarchy but it works because the onus is upon users to take care of others rather than assert their own rights.

Teenage boys and girls are physically familiar with each other in a close but innocent way. Compare this with the isolation many youths in the west face when left to entertain or even forage for themselves. Monitors responsible for group behaviour are drawn from peers – not older children. All children participate in regular sweeping and cleaning of the school premises. Teachers do provide supervisory duties but I have never seen them called upon to act and I have never seen a playground fight. All of this security means that they are superbly confident when dancing, singing or merely trying to answer questions in class, even when their grasp of the language is not so good. In fact it is this confidence in who they are and how and what their behaviour should be that most palpably strikes one when you observe relationships here. Compare this with the fragile egos of children in the west which need to be established and maintained by possession of the right designer labels to assert tribe membership and name-calling of those outside the tribe.

If there is a downside to all of this structure it is that there is an over-reliance on drills and exercise and not so much on creativity and imagination, something that new China badly needs. This is reflected in a school's own hierarchy which does not encourage any real sharing of experience or collaboration on projects. A sterile situation as quite often the principal may be a businessman and not a teacher. Allied to this and the whole idea of social networks is the concept of *guangxi* or connections. This is a system which ensures that jobs are given to people you are connected to, either socially or through family. So the strong social bonding that keeps society stable is also responsible for a weakening of good business and professionalism. Jobs and contracts are delivered to those who know each other or who meet and stoke each other up with drink. Given China's ripping growth the system can't be that bad but one feels that a meritocracy would be fairer to individuals and better for society.

Against the stunning growth seen in stock-market returns and ceaseless construction of luxury accommodation and new economic zones there remains a staidness which I suppose is the glue that holds all this together. The family is a sacred institution. Community too is important. In the heat of summer or the cold of winter men and women can be found in the streets of the cities or in the country sitting together, maybe talking or playing cards or even sitting alone – but still in the social milieu. The old religions are alive and people bow to the gods of Tao, Buddha and Christianity to ask for blessings on marriage and wealth. Pop music is here and art is breaking out of the traditional stylised scroll painting, but theatre is limited to singing and dancing spectaculars or traditional opera. Drama would be too progressive, too controversial. Similarly with literature, any unorthodox view will have to find a foreign publisher.

Helping to foster this stolidness in society there are strict rules about physical mobility; essentially people live, work and die where they are born as it is not possible to work or live outside the province of your birth. The exceptions to this include choices that can be made to work in the city where you graduate or which your spouse comes from. A stable population means that new ideas are not going to be flying around, unless from foreigners such as myself and we are very few. Stable but not uniform for secreted in the hills, valleys and towns of China's 1.3 billion are many ethnic minorities. In the west, in Latin America, in Africa this would inevitably be a problem sooner or later but in China they co-exist celebrating local customs, traditions and languages. Integrated perhaps because of the core nation-wide values of family and community.

Stolid too is the built environment. From villages of near identical single-story courtyard dwellings to cities of impersonal edifices. Even opulence here seems austere. This reinforces the feeling that social relationships take precedence over mere materialism; this is especially so of course for the many people who have only a single room to live in or even have to live in the room where they work. To be less romantic, it probably also reflects the fact that much of urban society is only one generation away from peasant farmer and there has been no tradition of comfort. Almost all settlements large or small are built on a North/South grid pattern. A physical paradigm for the sense that one always knows where one is in this society.

I can't comment on the media, the great leveller in 20th & 21st centuries, but I get the impression that it is not riven by debate, criticism or cutting-edge documentary and that TV producers "editorialise" if they want to stay in their jobs. A newspaper was shutdown recently and the editor imprisoned. A couple of films have recently been banned. The Rolling Stones were asked to omit some of their raunchier numbers in a recent concert. It is widely reported that there are 30,000 internet police – all part of China's great firewall. Google considered and then dropped proposals to be part of this. All of these measures prevent cultural contamination from new ideas and encourage the perpetuation of the old values without any question; for the UK imagine the sixties without hippies. However, companies such as KFC and McDonalds are in all major cities here and I am not clear how their brand of greedy commercialism together with the obesity and health problems fits in to what China wants to preserve. Sadly too, many advertisements feature representations of white Europeans in order to sell clothes or mobile phones.

As you would expect for such a self-assured lot, the Chinese have dignity. They dress smartly but not flashily whatever their position or wealth. Never have I seen so many straight backs and unwavering stares. I find myself becoming quite self-conscious when leaning against a vertical surface. The Chinese do not lounge or lean. They sit on low stalls and hard chairs or squat but they do not lounge. They move with deliberation and are physically fit; whether child or adult they know the body's limits.

As a blueprint for society it is very impressive; what a shame its values cannot be exported as easily as the cheap goods produced by its workers.

SUMMER HOLIDAY

Yet another plane journey. China is such a vast country that it would have taken days to get to our destination by train but my son Bredon had to be back in the kitchen where he worked in ten days and so we had to plan carefully to make the most of the time and wanted to spend as long as possible in the amazing places we were going to see - and the place we were going to was amazing. The landing approach seemed to betoken well as we followed a deep valley and then banked to port across richly vegetated terrain with dwellings on the edge of rivers which sported fishing boats dotted on them. The runway was lined on one side with a great bank of rocky hills which reared up sheer, one of which had a hole right through it.

We were at *Zhangjiajie* (jang-g-ar-jay), a wonderfully scenic area in *Hunan* province about 2000 miles west of *Weifang* which we had left for the last time after a week of farewells. Being a wonderfully scenic area it was something of a honeypot for tourists which in turn means there would be much advantage taking and over charging; I could see there was going to be a lot of bargaining ahead. The guidebook was mercifully clear about where we had to go; not *Zhangjiajie* City, but the village of the same name and there should be a bus to take us the 18 km or so. As we roved around the car park looking for suitable transport it was clear that we were too late for the public bus and the cloud of taxi-drivers which had followed us like flies trying to get our attention might be our best bet. We had ignored the first one who had grandly announced that he had been sent to collect us and listened to the selection of fares offered: 200 yuan – 150 – 110: we were in a strong position as there were several of them vying for our custom. Meanwhile the first one had managed to consolidate his position by finding an interpreter who made it known that he had actually been sent by the hotel we had booked. So far so good – I was happy enough to use hotel transport so we boarded it. The driver raced through the dwindling day along valleys with steep hills either side and occasionally plunging through long tunnels. The narrow margins were well cultivated.

As night fell we descended into the straggle of buildings that lined the village and drew up outside a pleasantly timbered building that was the hotel. As we checked in it transpired that payment for the "hotel transport" was still our responsibility. 150 yuan? – no I refused to pay more than the lowest fare that we had been quoted at the airport and given the distance that we had travelled that seemed to be fair; after some negotiation that proved to be acceptable.

Waking in the *Tujia* style room was a delight; the ceiling bore an intricate marquetry pattern and the walls were richly panelled. From the balcony overlooking the main street was a clear view of what we had come to see – the huge limestone pinnacles for which the area is famous. The plan was to trek around the park returning to *Zhangjiajie* village in three days time. Nobody seemed very keen on providing us with breakfast so we set off down the valley. First stop was to purchase some peaches and after some haggling we carried on to the park entrance. No haggling here! Whether we liked it or not park entrance was a massive 245 yuan for two days; that's what many workers earn in a week. The area thrives on tourism and it was at this point that a couple of local guides attached themselves to us with the pretence of helping us; it is easy for them to do this as most Chinese find it utterly inconceivable that any traveller would want to find their own way about a tourist attraction despite the fact that everything is usually well sign-posted and routes are laid out on well paved paths. The common sight at anywhere like this is a group of fifteen tourists with identifying baseball caps following a guide who yells out the virtues of the sights through a badly tuned megaphone. Sadly it does not occur to them to wander freely and reflect on the wonders individually.

Whilst the mass of people continued straight on we veered to the right amid protestations from our "guides". It was here that our breakfast was stolen. Approaching the gravelled upwards path we were too intent on getting the right route to notice the thieves but before we knew what had happened a troupe of Macao monkeys darted out and grabbed at the flimsy plastic bag that Bredon was carrying and in a moment the food we had bargained hard for was gone. Not a disaster but an irritation nevertheless.

If you have ever seen a traditional Chinese painting you will have seen it filled with impossibly vertical peaks sprouting with vegetation and issuing waterfalls which pour into the river which meanders around their bases. Pavilions nestle amongst them and people dwarfed by the peaks fish happily from boats on the river. I had spent the last year in China viewing these with profound scepticism. The geological formations were not possible, water would not behave naturally like that, trees could not grow there, artistic licence had been stretched to the limits. Yet here we were walking through exactly such a mythical landscape.

The gravelled track was broad and continued upwards with a valley to our left and a pass ahead. It seemed to serve the odd dwellings that we passed. It was mercifully free of people apart from a "guide" who had continued to dog our steps. Eventually, as politely as I could, I made it clear that we did not want him and he bid us farewell good-naturedly for the hour's walk back to the entrance to find a more likely suspect. With some relief we attained the summit and enjoyed the superb views before beginning the descent feeling fairly secure that we were on a good route. It is a strange thing in China but when cycling I had often taken a wide concrete road which seemed to promise an interesting destination only to find that it would end abruptly against a barrier of fields; others would slowly atrophy at first into narrower roads, then to mud roads then tracks which would finally get lost as paths between fields. Just after we passed a fairly substantial wooden building the crisp clean gravel disappeared and the track became mud-rutted and I had forebodings. Another fifteen minutes and the track terminated in a pile of timber with steep forested drops all around and a sheer wall the other side of the ravine. The only map we had showed the road going all of the way and the compass was not going to be of much help as routes in this type of terrain tended to have to take circuitous routes around obstacles so one would not always be going in the target direction. After casting around Bredon found a well-worn path descending through the woodland. With nothing to loose we plunged down and after about ten minutes arrived at a series of paths, bridges and steps. Choosing a direction – and luckily it turned out to be the right one – we then followed a most idyllic route: hot sun moderated by the tree cover, a stream to one side, giant black butterflies and the buzz-saw of unseen insects. I felt as if we had chanced on something private and special and much more interesting than the more public paths.

Over the next three days we saw the most astonishing sights; a narrow stairway that climbed through a narrow crack in the cliffs up and up until it dived through a tunnel and emerged on a high terrace. The view was of layer superimposed upon layer of peaks and spires vanishing into the heat-haze of the distance. Another crack in the rock gave on to a lake high above the valley floor with peaks all around and also within the lake which we boated around. On another day we followed a path which took us up and down the peaks. It was in a misty cloudscape so we moved with limited vision but sometimes there would be a gap and a vast depth would be revealed with spires above and below on the other side of a canyon wreathed in foliage and wispy cloud. On the final day we found a walkway set just below the rim of the cliff about a thousand feet above the valley floor and we walked through this most magical landscape. It is said that there are more than 3,000 spires in the scenic area. Some stand erect, some are tumbled and there is a couple which are actually joined high above the floor in a natural land bridge. The Buddhists have colonised this feature and the railings either side are completely laden with padlocks and red ribbons, each one a little token from a devotee to urge longevity or wealth or maybe fertility for themselves.

We came to the end of the walkway eventually and the route plunged down through the semi-tropical vegetation to the valley floor past souvenir shops and food shops. At the bottom, after the relative isolation of the places we had been seeing the sudden presence of tourists was an unwelcome intrusion. A monorail had been built and was shunting carriage-loads of people who were clustered round the vendors and drinks stalls. They took it in turns to stand in the favoured spots so that their existence in front of a particularly photogenic spire might be recorded. Maybe innocently, but I suspect as a marketing ploy, many of the more accessible spires had been given names according to what their shape suggested; so we would pass "Old Lady Picking A Flower" or "Angry Monkey". This was a feature of all Chinese tourist spots – the way in which the particular was promoted over the general, the way in which labels seemed more important than the reality, the way in which a preferred meaning was imposed on the consciousness. It made the tourist lazy and prevented him from opening his mind. *Zhangjiajie* possessed a unique drama and beauty, which was self-evident from even a cursory viewing. It was encouraging that so many people were drawn to it but depressing that once there they were content for their experience to be shaped by a rather tacky presumption. Or maybe the gorgeousness of the hard rock and ethereal mist was just too much for these city-dwellers and they could only appreciate it when re-packaged as a commodity. We fled alongside the monorail.

The *Yangzi* is 3,400 Km in length – the third longest river in the world. At one point in China it is actually called Long River. It rises on the bleak Tibetan plateau and flows out near Shanghai into the South China Sea. Like many rivers it is multifunctional: it is a navigational route and for about half of its length this includes substantial vessels: it is a recreational feature playing host to thousands of tourists each month: it is a source of water for millions of people: forty percent of the waste entering it is untreated so it is a rubbish dump and sewerage gutter too. The last of the concrete had been poured on the controversial dam of the three gorges project the week before we got there. I was expecting something grander. The Hoover Dam, for instance, forms an impressive curve bracing itself against the Colorado Canyon; from the roadway one looks at the trapped lake on one side and down, down, down hundreds of feet to the river itself on the other. The facts and figures I had heard about this one here were immense so by contrast, when faced with it, this dam was rather an anti-climax and it looked like a suburban wall. Nevertheless the vastness of the two sets of locks and the fury of the jet of water which issued from the dam did suggest a certain sense of scale. The arguments for the dam say that by controlling the flow, flooding lower down the river will be eradicated; it will produce a massive amount of hydro-electric energy which will rejuvenate the regional economy; by raising the river level upstream it will tame an unwieldy navigational channel. Unfortunately by raising the level upstream millions of people and their dwellings have had to be re-sited, sometimes forcibly and many historic artefacts have sunk below the flow. More exasperatingly the tonnes of soil washed down from Tibet and *Yunan* will slowly be deposited in the new lake to clog it completely, experts warn, in seventy years time. The Chinese answer is that there is plenty of time to discover a solution.

The boat – The Snow Mountain – had not been easy to find. Whilst all of the regular ferries tied up by the pleasant park fronting the river in *Yichang* (e-chang), ours was moored several kilometres beyond the city. It took four taxis to get from the station to the boat. One dropped us at the agent's office; one refused; one we jumped from after believing it to be going in the wrong direction and the last one needed to be guided in by mobile phone. Having found the boat and established that *Tsingdao* beer was an outrageous 25 yuan a can at the bar we found a shop at the mooring which was selling it at a quarter of the price and bought a sack full. As this was the low season the boat was carrying only a fraction of its total passengers so life on board was very pleasant and life revolved around the meals and shore trips. On one of these a steamer took us along a tributary where we transferred to small craft rowed by six men. As the river became narrower and shallower progress became slower. Eventually five of the men leapt out and attached themselves to a long hemp rope and continued to tow the boat bent almost parallel to the shingle beach straining against the current. They were clothed of course but traditionally had been naked because the shirts that they wore in the past were made of a material that chafed their skin when the straining rope was applied to them. After continuing like this for some time we had gone as far as we were going and they leapt back into the boat which turned around and we made a much quicker descent over rapids and fast channels. At some time in the past these boats would have taken goods and people to destinations up and down river, but now they bore fat tourists on this fairground ride of an excursion. The tourists were happy and so were the boatmen who earned a good fee; they had gone through hard times when other forms of transport had taken over from them, before the tourists arrived.

This part of the *Yangzi* is famously known for its three gorges and they were seriously impressive even now, as the water rose, that they were not as deep. What did we see from the decks? Tall interlocking cliffs, tracks sometimes following the river bank, earth-movers attempting remedial work on the steep crumbling river side, and often great sheets of re-inforcing concrete, metal and stone. Sometimes we would encounter whole cities newly built with millions of souls strangely unseen, sometimes small villages of mud and thatch clinging to a single road above the river. This was a mining area and often there were enormous bunkers down the steep slopes into which trucks discharged their loads which in turn discharging the filthy coal to the lighters that tied up alongside, the whole process determined by gravity and the whole area blackened by the activity. The river was constantly, maniacally active with large cargo and passenger ships: at the side we saw ferries, some of them built to take three trucks abreast and shipbuilders putting the finishing touches to yet more vessels. As we got nearer to our destination and thus further from the dam the full force of the river current became apparent. We overhauled ships painfully slowly, their engines seemingly not even able to stem the current, and when we took a bend in the river the enormous boat would slew round as the raging current hit the side and we progressed crab-wise for a time. On the other hand boats going in the other direction, downstream sped by with a dangerous and indecent speed. The entire section must have been an exciting proposition when it had been its original one hundred metres lower complete with submerged rocks and shallows and rapids.

Chongqing (shong-shing), our destination, was another Chinese city, but this time with the distinction of being the fastest-growing city in the world. At some point in this year 2006, a peasant would enter this city to find work, a home and a new life and the world would tip from having predominantly a rural population to being predominantly urban. The ship leaving presented a dilemma for me. The previous day an envelope had appeared in our cabin with a slip of paper proclaiming that if we had been happy with the service it was customary to leave a tip – one for the staff in general and another in particular for the guide. I had no complaints about the service and standard of care which was excellent, but this was China and one did not tip in China, nor had I budgeted for it; also the trip had been expensive enough anyway by Chinese norms although probably not by European ones. Our next destination was the giant Buddha carved out of the rock at *Leshan*.

At seventy-six metres this was an impressive piece of sculpture and well worth the detour. The red sandstone figure gazed impassively down on the treacherous confluence of rivers he had been constructed to make safe. As with every tourist site not only were there stairways and viewing platforms serving the buddha himself but a whole warren of pagodas, temples cafes and restaurants strewn over the hillside. A pleasant enough way to spend the day. The town itself was on the opposite side of the river and made all the more attractive for having an extensive river frontage lined with cafes and bars – something one is used to in Europe but not often found here. We made the most of it as our next stop would be *Chengdu* where Bredon would fly home and I would fly to Tibet.

TIBET

Dancing at 30,000 feet? I'm usually impervious to Strange Things That Happen When You Travel but this seemed just a little too surreal for words and I wondered whether to wake my travelling companions so that they could share the spectacle. I didn't and they wished that I had! In every other way the Sichuan Airways flight was like all others, but then, forty minutes before touchdown a highly costumed stewardess appeared, the videoscreens flickered to life with views of the Tibetan terrain and the music began. As you will appreciate the configuration of seating on an aeroplane limits physical expression to a north/south direction which would challenge even a world-class choreographer but nevertheless the dancer danced gracefully with delicate hand movements and a beautiful smile. Gracefully - despite the passengers ducking under her hands on their way to the toilet, or the occasional turbulence; as she finished she received a well-deserved round of applause.

Gonkhar airport at 3,700 metres is an apt introduction to the roof of the world in a great basin of snow-capped mountains. The road to *Lhasa*, the capital, is a strenuous 90 Km away across wide raging rivers, through tunnels and over the Tibetan plateau. Tibetan dwellings appeared as we reached the City. These are quite special. Flat-roofed, stone-built, walls inward leaning. Windows outlined with a painted trapezoidal black frame and porches fringed with hanging fabric. On the outskirts we could see the biggest monastery in Tibet, *Drepung*, half way up the northern bank of the mountains. As they closed in and rural became urban the expected Chinese building lined the wide highway at first utilitarian and then bombastic with shops and restaurants which were clones of everything seen elsewhere in the Chinese mainland.

Tibet and China have had a close and stormy relationship for hundreds of years. Its altitude and ring of mountains has determined its geographical separateness that has led to the development of a separate language and culture. In 1951 following Mao's success in ousting all opponents from mainland China and establishing his People's Republic, the Chinese army marched into Tibet to "liberate" it. Now it is debatable that anyone at that time desired to be "liberated" but on the other hand the country was ruled in a feudal style with all the trappings of serfdom and bond-slavery that that implies. Foreigners were mostly prohibited from entering the country, trade was limited, living conditions were miserable, sanitation and potable water were rare. The penal system was unjust and harsh. Secular education was absent, electricity and paved roads were rare. A treaty was signed and an uneasy relationship opened the way for creeping Chinese incursion which brought the twentieth century to Tibet. This lasted until the end of the fifties when the Chinese, never very easy with the power of the monasteries, precipitated the flight of the chosen leader, the Dalai Lama to India. The gloves were off. In eighteen months between 1959 and 1960 87,000 people were killed and a further ten percent starved as a result of the ill-thought out agricultural policies of Mao's Great Leap Forward. 130,000 Tibetans fled to *Dharamsala* in India to form a government in exile. The reality today is a very strong military presence: checkpoints on roads abound, army convoys clog the roads, soldiers are to be found at posts by shops, hotels and pedestrian ways. More damaging perhaps is the massive influx of Chinese who run the smart shops and travel agents bringing with them their own culture and expectations continually diluting the history and culture of the indigene.

One feature difficult to dilute is the *Potala Palace*. *Lhasa* is set in a valley bowl of the Himalayas and in the centre of this is a massive granite hill and clothing the top and sides of this is the enormous palace built in thirteen stories with over a thousand rooms. This must be one of the world's most beautiful buildings mostly white but topped with a section finished in a deep terracotta red, the whole graceful structure moulded on the contours of the hill and visible from anywhere in the city. We passed the palace and after a block further east found ourselves in old *Lhasa*. Stone structures replaced the glass and concrete. Large display windows were replaced with narrow lock-up stores, some with counters across the openings, selling directly onto the street. From the main street alleys crammed with stalls led back into the depths of traditional *Lhasa*. Dwellings are found in enormous communal structures built around courtyards, arranged around galleries sometimes with a temple in the middle. Self-contained communities. As in many parts of China sanitation is limited so the smell of urine is never far away and one may see children defecating in a corner of the street. On the street too the carcasses of yaks lie in great blooded heaps having been unloaded from the groaning trucks while they are waiting to be butchered.

Rows of shops dedicated to yak meat reek of blood and offal, others have great rounds of yak butter piled up on wooden shelves. Otherwise in shops you will find what you will find anywhere – vegetables, fruit, clothes, furniture. In the alleyways all of this produce is more immediately present piled plentifully high on the stalls. Some such as the hardware stalls, have a dazzling variety of items for sale, all packed away each evening and then lovingly arranged each new day. Some incorporate stoves to cook fried potatoes and other tasty morsels. The alleys themselves seem to follow no pattern and are impossible to map. They curve serpent-like, take sudden changes of direction and end in courtyard gateways. Getting to a destination is a matter of good fortune not logic. One clear focus for many is the *Barkhor kora*. This is a rough circuit around the most holy of Tibetan temples, the *Jokhang*. Tucked away off this concourse are many other temples and next to one is a prison museum. This is a true curiosity. Cells are embedded in each of the four walls with mannequins in chains posed in grotesque postures to illustrate the degradations suffered by Tibetans under their pre-Chinese leaders. Crude propaganda forces the message home - with tales of eyes being gouged out and limbs removed – that life here used to be grim, wretched and dangerous. If one accepts that the pot is calling the kettle black here it is worth remembering that between three hundred thousand and a million Tibetans have perished since the "liberation" either directly or indirectly, and there are said to be presently between six and seven hundred political detainees.

None of this is visible however and apart from the strong military presence and the need for permits to travel to and within Tibet life appears to be peaceable and civilised. Back on the *kora* the stalls are packed with tourist gewgaws and the way is packed with many pilgrims all moving in a clockwise direction. Some walk briskly swinging their prayer wheels, others progress in a dance of prostration: hands joined above heads and then falling first to knees and then hands sliding flat along the ground. To understand these rituals one must accept the concept of "merit" in the Buddhist world. Various deeds endow the doer with merit which move them up the evolutionary level in the next life. Walking the *kora*, spinning the prayer wheels, praying, giving offerings, all apparently ensure the transition from peasant to monk or abbot. As there can only be a finite number of abbots or Dalai Lamas the competition to acquire merit is fierce unless all of these pilgrims are already on their way to nirvana – the ultimate state of existence.

Tibet is saturated by religion: turn a corner and you are confronted by a temple; walk a street and every other person will be armed with a prayer wheel; monks sit begging at the side of the road; look at the surrounding mountains and you will see great hawsers of prayer flags heaving in the wind. The great glories of the country apart from the wilderness terrain are the monasteries. Some are tiny with just a few monks such as the one at *Namtso* one hundred and seventy kilometres north of *Lhasa*. This is one of the holy places, an enormous salt-water lake at 4,700 metres. At one end on the shore are three huge boulders and beside them a cave has been enclosed to accommodate images of the Buddha. This is one of Tibet's smaller temples with a handful of monks. From the hill above views of the lake are massively impressive: still, unreal blue with nothing on it at all, and snow-capped mountains around which slope down to the shore – again with no sign of human presence. The sky races with clouds of all hues broken at times with the high sun and a sky that matches the blue of the lake.

At the other end of the spectrum are the great monasteries *of Shigatse, Serpa, Ganden and Drepung*. This last one rambles all over the mountains to the west of *Lhasa* and is home to about six hundred monks, who rattle around buildings designed for ten thousand. The kitchen which was designed to serve this number still possesses the giant wood-fired cauldrons that are still in use They are so big that they have to be stirred by garden spades and whisks driven by power drills while copper serving vessels gleam in ranks against the walls. Outside buildings are littered at random all over the steep arid hillside connected by earth tracks or steps. Plunge inside the temples along with the pilgrims and there is a riot of colour everywhere. Most of the wall surface is richly decorated with paintings of Buddha representations. In the larger assembly halls the roof is supported by hundreds of elaborately decorated wooden pillars with light coming from clerestory windows high above streaming down through woven tapestries, some formed into large cylinders hanging over the floor below. The surrounding walls are pierced with doors leading to chapels of varying significance crammed with effigies which may be of past revered leaders, but more often represent the multifarious faces of the Buddha, at peace, in anger as an animal or as a demon, with many arms or heads. Some chapels may have larger-than-life images – at *Shigatse* the statues are 26 metres high; some have rows and rows of identical tiny statuettes. Generally represented as sitting cross-legged they are clothed richly and may be flanked by attendants. Outside the large assembly halls other chapels are to be found in the maze of buildings which are part of any monastery complex accessed through courtyards, narrow alleys or up narrow staircases. Pilgrims, always moving around the chapels in a clock-wise direction, constantly intone in a low murmur and make offerings to each image. The offerings range from foodstuffs, to yak butter replenishment for the illuminating candles but more often money. Every surface around the chapels is littered and every crack is crammed with low-value currency, usually one jiao which is worth about a halfpenny, and each one is donated in the hope of earning merit along the road to nirvana. In some chapels a framework of chicken-wire has been set up to accept the money and the rolled notes populate the wire in a way that would not look out of place as an exhibit in a gallery of modern art. One of the functions of the monks is to collect these notes and change them with each influx of pilgrims who then redistribute them around the chapels with dedicated earnestness.

The atmosphere in all of these chapels from the largest assembly hall to the smallest is one of quiet gloom even when the more popular destinations such as the *Jokhang* in the middle of *Lhasa* are crammed with pilgrims. There is always a brisk sense of purpose attached to visiting the holy shrines and making the appropriate obeisance or offering and moving on. Pilgrims hustle around the *Koras*, they spin the giant prayer wheels and duck into alcoves. It all seems business-like and pragmatic and lacking in gravity or awe but completely obsessive. *Ganden* monastery is rather wonderfully perched on a hilltop summit about an hour from *Lhasa*. The pilgrim bus returning from it suddenly stopped at a minor monastery. "Emergency prayer stop!" quipped one of my fellow travellers.

The atmosphere in a more literal sense in all of the chapels is saturated by yak butter; candles singly or in great tureens burn yak butter; the fumes of burning butter are in the air; monks and pilgrims heave jugs of the stuff to keep them burning; hand rails are tacky; the floors are sticky with it. In the ante-chamber in front of the *Jokhang* are thousands of yak butter candles kept burning all day by four attendants; put your hand on the exterior wall and the accumulated heat is surprisingly evident.

I met with one young nun in a lesser monastery on the outskirts of *Lhasa* who explained how the system worked. Her room like any western student's was filled with books and pictures. Nuns and monks are viewed by the Chinese as potential trouble. During the Cultural Revolution between 1966-1976 2,700 monasteries were destroyed in Tibet and their inhabitants scattered, imprisoned or killed. In order to prove their allegiance to the new regime nuns and monks have to take an exam and according to their answers they are paid a salary by the state. The "wrong" answers could lead to imprisonment. Imprisonment will inevitably follow any demonstration of allegiance to the Dalai Lama in *Dharamasala* and all references to him including his photograph are banned. When I point out that she has an incriminating photograph of the Dalai Lama on her wall she shrugs and tells me that they are warned when the police come to make a search. But two of her friends are currently in prison. She is very sanguine about her situation and tells me that the police – who are fellow Tibetans – usually give notice of any visit. They tread a difficult line. The tension which exists between China and monasteries is compounded by the fact that the monasteries are being farmed by the Chinese for their tourist potential; entrance fees, which are often more than a week's wage for some Tibetans are in line with what Western tourists can afford. The money goes to the Chinese. Up and down the length of the country monasteries are being rebuilt and repaired to ensure revenue. One could say that the monks and nuns have sold out, but they have little choice.

At *Serpa*, another large foundation to the north of *Lhasa*, the monks meet every afternoon to debate faux philosophy. At 3.00 a bell rings and the heavy red doors to a shady courtyard are opened and in pour monks from all over the monastery. In pairs one will sit and the other will stand. The standing monk will put a question and then with a curious glancing clap and violent out thrust of one leg will challenge the other to respond. It seems that this is not a journey to establish truth but a way of examining each other in the scriptures, and to judge from the shouts of triumph to catch each other out. The age of the monks ranged from eleven to over sixty. There is a suggestion that all of this activity is a natural release in the daily round of sitting and contemplation. The whole courtyard, the trees, the white stone and the vivid crimsons of the robes and the animated chatter is a tremendous spectacle, which makes for a great tourist event which one suspects is increasingly the raison d'être for the daily debate.

To appreciate the appeal of the religion you have to frame it within a combination of wretched poverty and pre-TV sophistication. For the average peasant who has maybe travelled far from their simple dwelling there is something utterly compelling about the fantasy embodied by the monasteries. As the men and women shuffle along the well-trodden routes there is expectation with every plunge into scented gloom and a magic in the sudden way that the next image is revealed. The unworldly features or sumptuous clothing of the statues illuminated by flickering candles or sometimes dramatically lit by carefully positioned windows. It serves a function not unlike that of an old-fashioned peep show or latter day theme park attraction. Remember, the daily life and environment of the average Tibetan is mean and wretched, with little comfort and no colour. The theatricality of all of this and the richly coloured paintings on the walls are as compulsive to the Tibetans as the glitzy music halls were to the Victorian proletariat. If the belief system says that simply by visiting one of these palaces and performing some rudimentary rituals you can better your spiritual and physical well-being it is going to be a winner. It is also a form of social control of course. On an immediate level as long as the majority of the population subscribe to the belief system stability is assured. But the cunning move is to endow the monkhood with an elevated status that makes it attractive to mostly young men – the very segment of the population that traditionally might want to upset the status quo. Families with many children and too little land or too few yak to distribute can have a clear conscience in sending their sons to be educated – I use the word advisedly – in a revered institution.

Unlike the safety-obsessed west hardly anything in any of these buildings is off limits so one is often wandering into private accommodation or onto roofs with unprotected edges up precipitous steps. I'd often had time to ruminate on how the buildings managed to remain waterproof – flat roofs and no asphalt or plastic membrane in sight. Entering a chapel one day my question was answered; a rhythmic beating and men's and women's voices which I initially assumed to be part of the ritual. I followed my ears up a set of steps and came upon a work group. Eight men and eight women in formation each with a flattened stone on the end of a pendant stick their trousers spattered with cement. The concrete had been laid and was still damp. The song was a calling song – question and answer – between the men and the women. The feet and the stones were being used rhythmically to tamp down the setting mixture and compact it. Singing, stamping, moving slightly, singing, stamping. In that hot Himalayan sun I do not think that modern machines and modern methods could ever replace the camaraderie or good humour of those sixteen workers.

When I subsequently learned that the marmot is the primary carrier of the bubonic plague carrying flea I was doubly grateful that we had not tackled the Ganden/Samye trail. Three or four days trekking over high Tibetan passes from one famous monastery to another seemed wonderful. As is the way I had done the rounds of the tourist agencies but I eventually came into contact with my fellow travellers through advertisements on the hotel notice boards and through chance meeting. However, when we turned up at the hotel ready to go it was then that we discovered that the trail was off-limits. The official explanation was that the marmots had flu; as this was in the middle of the avian flu scare it was a credible explanation although I had heard a rumour that there was political unrest in the area too.

So it was that with some quick thinking with suggestions from *Tashi* our guide that our revised route would start at *Tsurphu* and our starting point was a couple of hours north of *Lhasa*. On the way we passed a small truck whose frame had been squeezed into a parallelogram by a landslide and this reminded us that this was the rainy season – season of sudden deluges and cataracts from unexpected quarters. It was also a season, at the moment anyway, of bright, warm sunshine. Taking the dirt track off the main highway we followed the valley. At one point we came to a work party centred around a couple of small buildings. In one of them barley was being roasted and in the other it was being milled by water driven stones. In between the two the roasted grain was being winnowed by groups of peasants. A scene out of eighteenth century Europe.

As we arrived at *Tsurphu* monastery two things happened. One - the weather broke treacherously into a downpour and two – a brightly coloured procession emerged from the building. Garbed in red and yellow the procession bearing drums and horns made their way to the river. Thirty or so monks were there, some with head-dresses like monstrous mohicans, some like giant open butterfly wings, some carrying flags, some carrying totems, some clashing cymbals. As they arrived at the bridge over the torrent the entourage arranged themselves some on one side and some on the other. The chief celebrant took his place in the middle of the wooden bridge and with what seemed a little indecision performed the ritual in what had now developed into a healthy wind and rain. Facing upstream he poured what I

113

assumed to be holy water and grain into the white water below. With some drumming and blowing the ceremony was soon over and the procession, garments flapping in the wind, made its way back to the monastery.

After lunch in the monastery kitchen and a swift look around we set up camp on the track further upstream. We were sited just below the sky burial place. For reasons of economy, practicality and tradition Tibetans enjoy a different method of disposal to Westerners. After due ceremony bodies are left on the stony tract to be consumed by the birds of the air – principally by vultures. This is encouraged by the removal of the corpse's hands and feet. The idea of your body being elevated and recycled in this way is a truly spiritual and not unpleasant one I believe. Buddhist dignitaries, however, may be treated to a cremation their ashes preserved in a monastery shrine to be honoured by monks and pilgrims.

The following day while waiting for our porters and yaks to arrive we ascended the cliff above the monastery to explore the warren of dwellings and hermitages. Some were under reconstruction, but they all had marvellous views over the valley and down to the monastery below. In one a nun of sixty-five was resident and had been so for over eleven years. She had not moved from this place in all of this time. I asked why an area between four upright pillars had been cordoned off. This was a sacred space in which her devotions led her to see the gods dancing. Another collection of buildings was completely forbidden to us. These housed a dozen or so monks who were on a serious quest for spiritual enlightenment. They were incarcerated for three years, three months and three days with the only outside contact being a cook. They spent their time in prayer and meditation and it was said that such was the power of their devotion that they were able to levitate.

Time for us to levitate, and after descending the cliff we made our way up the valley. It was immediately apparent that this was at last a remote part of the country. No dwellings, no farming, only rough paths alongside the river becoming slimmer as we forged higher. Imagine Wales only two miles higher. We walked all afternoon in such terrain until high up we came to a junction and took the left-hand fork. Moving up the steep slope we eventually caught sight of the tents which had been taken on ahead and had been erected for us. The campground was a curious pockmarked surface and when I paused to look I saw why. Hundreds of small creatures – hamsters – lived in these holes and were darting between them seemingly oblivious to us. Not only hamsters but also humans. Above our camp on a ledge were a tent and a stone dwelling. The inevitable children were already gathering around our tents and showed great interest in our bags and possessions and of course, our cameras. With dark skins and a motley collection of clothes they formed handsome subjects and were eager to see the digital images of themselves – quite a novelty in a mirror-free environment. The eldest, a boy of about twelve, displayed his prowess to me in using the sling that cracked satisfyingly as the stone hurtled at an unwitting hamster – which escaped. He also took me to his home. The tent he invited me to was very different to mine. I had already been told that the Tibetans did not believe in comfort. A large rectangular space was covered by the tent which was shaped like a hipped roof. My tent was a close-woven fabric waterproofed and designed to keep out wind and weather. This was yak hair woven very roughly through which the daylight entered and which would also allow the rain and night winds to enter. The whole structure defined a space rather than provided shelter. Within the space were two steel bed frames, some shelves, a wooden chest of drawers and a cupboard. At one end was a stove. All on the bare floor. My young friend offered me some water which he poured from a vacuum flask into some barely clean cups.

The next day's walking was climactic. The reason that Tibetans can run around all day is because their bodies have adjusted to the altitude. They have larger lung capacity and more oxygen-carrying red blood corpuscles. Westerners from lower altitudes can develop the latter but it takes time and after a week at altitude I was still finding physical effort difficult. On this day we managed two 5,000 metre passes – slowly. I was extremely glad that for this trek everything was being carried by the yaks. The sense of achievement at being at such an altitude through my own efforts and was reinforced by the visibly dramatic evidence around me. Mountain peaks in an untidy series disappeared into the distance, clouds brushed them dividing and reforming, below on either side of the watershed the nascent streams flowed away. No body and no human evidence could be seen anywhere. Achievement is rarely so sweet or hard won.

We had been following one valley after another but on the next day we came out of a valley onto a spectacular arena. Like high moorland with mountains on every side but also with valleys below us clearly showing the routes of rivers and tributaries. After two days of tough walking this gave a tremendous lift to our spirits. Our route took us to a fast-flowing river too wide to ford, but as if by some private arrangement a girl on horseback appeared who was prevailed upon to lead us across. Unfortunately when her father appeared he insisted that we doubled the fee that we had agreed with the daughter. Eventually we arrived at our destination, the nunnery at *Yangbajing*. Looking down on the buildings nestled under the cliffs opposite us it bore a certain resemblance to the cliff dwellings of the First People I had seen in the United

States – a sort of organic growth erupting from the valley ledge.

This was where we rejoined our transport and headed back to Lhasa, but not before stopping at another curiosity. After driving along the valley which widened out into a gravely expanse we saw in the distance columns of steam rising in the mountain air. This was the geothermal power station. Next to it was the geothermal swimming pool fed by the hot springs. What an amazing experience it is to swim breathlessly at 4,300 metres in the open air, in water faintly smelling of sulphur with a bank of snow-capped mountains on one side. Out of this world.

Mist covers the valley at *Rongbuk* at eight in the morning. I walk past the monastery with the angry flowing river to my right. There is no vegetation, just chill rock and boulders. Behind is the road to *Lhasa* and *Khatmandu*, the hotel and the guest house and the car park filled with 4x4s, one of which brought me here over dirt roads and mountain passes. Ahead is the highest mountain in the world but I cannot see it. It was overcast when we arrived last night and although it is brighter this morning the cloud is low. Ever hopeful I keep checking the valley sides to determine if I can see a little further up and so judge if the cloud is lifting. I am pleased to be here whatever the visibility but I would really like to see the summit. The noise of the river is loud. The track is rising at one point up a zigzag to over five thousand metres and by nine o'clock I am certain that the cloud is lifting. I find a small hill where some others are already standing and where I can look up the valley past base-camp to the mountain. We don't have to wait long and the view is not one hundred per cent at any one time but between the moving shrouds I can reconstruct the massive white delicate shape. I can see the ridges and gullies without knowing their names. I can see the moraine a couple of kilometres away and imagine climbers encountering this on their way to the great challenge. It is pyramidal from this angle with a spur in the foreground and what looks like horizontal ledges below the summit. It is sailing a sea of snow and cloud. The whole scene is whited with cloud and snow with the bare rock texture of the mountain showing through and giving it form like a two-dimensional scraperboard image. It is both easy and difficult to believe that the top is a three thousand metre – nearly two miles - vertical ascent from where I am.

Hardly taking my eyes from the magic I move on to base camp, a village of tent hotels and tent shops present all year but occupied fully during the early and late summer periods when climbing conditions are at their optimum. Hotel California, Hotel Yak & Yeti, Snowland Guesthouse advertise the tents. Trinkets for the daytime tourists. A China Post office charging an outrageous amount for sending a postcard. Everything here needs to be trucked in and trucked out along two hundred kilometres of dirt roads. There is nothing here apart from a tent village and rock and snow but the romance and challenge of the place is palpable and my eyes keep being drawn to the mountain: *Chomolungma* in Tibetan, *Zhumulangma* in Chinese, Everest. I have no desire to climb it myself – that's too much danger and hardship – but to be somewhere which is unique and which has drawn so many people to it and which must be surely known by every educated person that walks the earth. I feel privileged to have been able to make this journey.

The way back to *Lhasa* was far more prosaic. Narrow steep sided valleys which we climbed in the straining car on tracks which were uncomfortably narrow when we had to pass another vehicle. Small villages with narrow streets next to rivers. Up up to the high passes festooned with prayer flags where everyone stops and which attract the vendors, some supplying decorated yaks to sit on for photographs. The view back was all brown rolling waves at first then shadowed and finally in the distance a band of black summits snow-touched and one of them Everest.

This is also the road to *Khatmandu*, a well-travelled route, and progress is being made on surfacing it. In the middle of nowhere whole villages of workers live for months in the inhospitable terrain while working on the new road. They could be seen up to their arms in concrete or shifting boulders or operating machinery. We would come to whole sections of completed road and speed along it then it would suddenly end and we would have to find our way on makeshift detours over the churned mud. On one occasion we had to start at 6.30 in the morning because the whole section was a one-way route for a twelve hour stretch and the switch in directions was at 7.00. On another a policed barrier was down with a queue of trucks in front of us. We simply backed off and found a diversion around the barrier past stone cottages and driving through streams and over rough ground before regaining the road. 4x4s – such monstrous underuse in the suburbs of the west but coming into their own here! On one zigzag route down a hill the driver suddenly swung off the track bypassing it – by driving vertically downhill. Our driver, a friendly man, was a chain-smoker and, unable to smoke in the car, suggested frequent toilet/viewing/lunch/stretch-our-legs stops as a thin excuse to give him the opportunity to satisfy his craving.

Near habitations or at obvious stopping points men and women and children would gather round the vehicle out of curiosity or to sell fruit or trinkets. Some of them had fossils to sell, searched for and hewn from their locality; many of them offered attractive geodes in which a lump of rock is split to reveal the perfect form of a fossilised shell or other creature. They bargained hard for their sales – they knew the value of them. Amazingly in a country that must have so few consumer goods rubbish was a real problem. I could be miles from anywhere and yet be walking on trash –discarded plastic bags were common and, unaccountably, shoes. It was as if their former owners had made a point of travelling along that path in order to dispose of them. One would think that here was a simple people leading simple lives and having few of the problems of the west but I had met this problem in the Amazon jungle too. Of course what happens is that these simple people dispose of their rubbish in the traditional way by flinging it onto the land which is vast and traditionally able to absorb it because of a low density population and because it is largely organic. Unfortunately now the land can cope with neither the influx of tourists nor the undegradeable trash. Such as plastic bottles. I was stretching my legs within the Everest National Park during one of our many fag-stops when a bottle whizzed past my ear. Unbelievingly I picked it up and returned it to its owner, a university educated airport worker from Shanghai who was travelling with me. I am not sure whether his apologies were for the act or for the shame of being shown up by a westerner.

The road from Everest was also the start of the road home and once back in *Lhasa* I tied up final travel arrangements. By-passing the agents who told me there were no tickets available I took a taxi to the station and bought myself a ticket for 523 yuan to *Xining*, from where I would fly to *Beijing*. Having failed to secure a train ticket coming into Tibet I was very pleased about this because this was a brand new railway, less than a month old. The railway is a matter of technological pride for the Chinese who have completed it well before schedule. More importantly the *Qinghai-Tibet* railway is now the longest plateau railway with the highest elevation in the world and is laid over some of the most difficult terrain. The engineering feats include a bridge nearly twelve kilometres long and the world's longest frozen soil tunnel. The construction has had to deal with hundreds of river crossings, animal migrations and huge temperature ranges. Most of the track is laid on a fenced embankment with tunnels under it to ensure animal movements are not disrupted. Environmentalists warn that the railway might degrade the delicate sub-surface and there is news that this is already happening. What is certain though is that it will encourage tourism and trade in the area. The massive influx of Chinese – three or four train loads daily – will further dilute and erode what is left of Tibetan culture. I foresee *Namtso*, the lake that I visited, gloriously blue and uninhabited now, in another five years filled with pleasure craft, hotels bordering it. Or the "Scenic Area of *Tsurphu*" with guides leading Chinese tourists around the sky-burial site and the hermitages – reached by cableways. The region I fear is set to become a cultural theme park with all the detritus that that entails.

I was nonetheless happy to use the facilities in my "hard-sleeper" on the train. Air-conditioned with oxygen-supply for anyone suffering from altitude sickness and a comfortable bunk I could watch the wild and remote landscape slide past the windows. A narrow valley to start with but mostly the high plateau at around five thousand metres – lakes, marsh, sand with a thin covering of vegetation. In the distance snow-capped mountains. Occasionally the tents of nomads and their yaks and the odd train stop in towns with some strategic purpose such as a fuel depot or military centre. I was not aware of any insurgency form the Free-Tibet campaign but strangely at about kilometre intervals there were soldiers standing to attention in the hot sun at the side of the rail. The train's progress was constant though not fast. The view was compulsive. I let the beauty and the monotony sustain me throughout the journey, the wilderness below echoed by big skies above; lake marsh and sand.

Printed in the United Kingdom
by Lightning Source UK Ltd.
119464UK00001B/230